The Essential Book of
EMBROIDERY STITCHES

100+ STITCHES WITH STEP-BY-STEP PHOTOS AND EXPLANATIONS

ATELIER FIL
HIROKO SEI AND SHIZUE YASUI

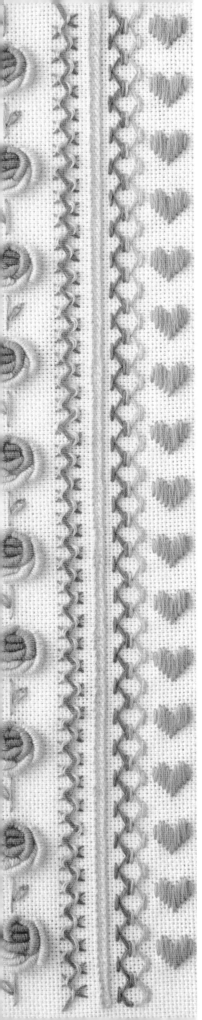

CONTENTS

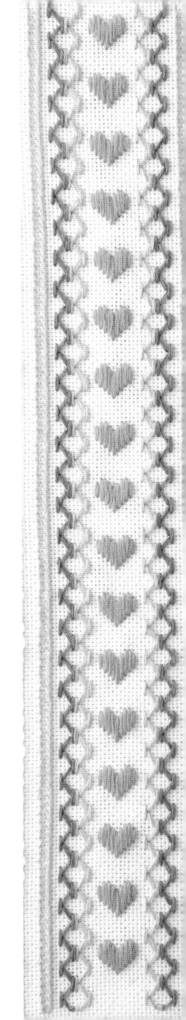

INTRODUCTION

For over 2000 years, embroidery has been passed down through the generations. This art-form was initially developed to make and embellish clothing. Most of the stitches we know today have a long history. The technique and the name used for some similar stitches can vary depending on the period and the country. In this book we present traditional techniques. Embroidery work, like all handicraft requires time. I hope you will discover the pleasure of embroidery and that you will enjoy creating your own original designs.

ATELIER FIL
HIROKO SEI AND SHIZUE YASUI

STITCH INDEX

Line Stitches

Running Stitch P.18	Whipped Running Stitch P.19	Laced Running Stitch P.19	Holbein Stitch P.20
Darning Stitch P.20	Back Stitch P.21	Whipped Back Stitch P.22	Laced Back Stitch P.22
Pekinese Stitch P.23			
Outline Stitch P.24	Outline Filling P.27	Zigzag Stitch P.27	Couching P.28
Split Stitch P.29			
Chain Stitch P.30	Whipped Chain Stitch P.32	Laced Chain Stitch P.32	Open Chain Stitch P.33
Chain Filling P.33			
Cable Chain Stitch P.34	Twisted Chain Stitch P.35	Checkered Chain Stitch P.36	Fly Stitch P.37
Buttonhole Stitch P.38			
Tailor's Buttonhole Stitch P.39	Closed Buttonhole Stitch P.40	Double Buttonhole Stitch P.41	Buttonhole Wheel P.41
Up and Down Buttonhole Stitch P.42			
Feather Stitch P.43	Double Feather Stitch P.44	Closed Feather Stitch P.45	Single Feather Stitch P.46
Cretan Stitch P.46			

Open Cretan Stitch P.47	Herringbone Stitch P.48	Shadow Work P.48	Closed Herringbone Stitch P.49	Laced Herringbone Stitch P.49
Double Herringbone Stitch P.50	Herringbone Ladder Stitch P.50	Cable Plait P.51	Rosette Chain Stitch P.51	Fishbone Stitch P.52
Raised Fishbone Stitch P.53	Leaf Stitch P.53	Chevron Stitch P.54	Vandyke Stitch P.55	

Filling Stitches

Straight Stitch P.57	Seed Stitch P.57	Satin Stitch P.58	Long and Short Stitch P.60	Lazy Daisy Stitch P.62
Double Lazy Daisy Stitch P.62	Tulip Stitch P.63	Ring Stitch P.63	French Knot P.64	French Knot with Tail P.65
German Knot P.66	Cable Stitch P.67	Danish Knot P.68	Colonial Knot P.68	Plain Knot P.69
Four-Legged Knot P.24	Bullion Stitch P.70	Bullion Rose P.72	Bullion Knot P.73	Bullion Daisy P.73

5

Spider Web Rose P.74	Ribbed Spider Web P.75	Cast-On Stitch P.76	Basket Filling P.78	Honeycomb Filling P.79
Cloud Filling P.79	Wave Filling P.79	Twisted Lattice Filling P.80	Trellis Couching P.81	Jacobean Couching P.81

Cross Stitch

Cross Stitch P.82	Half Cross Stitch P.85	Double Cross Stitch P.85	Three Quarter Cross Stitch P.85	

Stumpwork

Corded Detached Buttonhole Stitch P.88	Buttonhole Bar P.90	Detached Buttonhole Stitch P.91	Raised Stem Stitch P.94	Raised Chain Stitch P.95

Ceylon Stitch P.96	Turkey Work P.97	Raised Leaf Stitch P.98	**Drawn Thread Work** Hem Stitch P.104	Knotted Border P.105

Hardanger

Interlaced Border P.106	Needle Weaving P.107	Overcast Bar P.108	Four Sided Stitch P.108	Satin Stitch P.110
Eyelet Stitch P.110	Woven Bars P.112	Dove's Eye P.112	Picots P.113	Buttonhole Stitch P.114

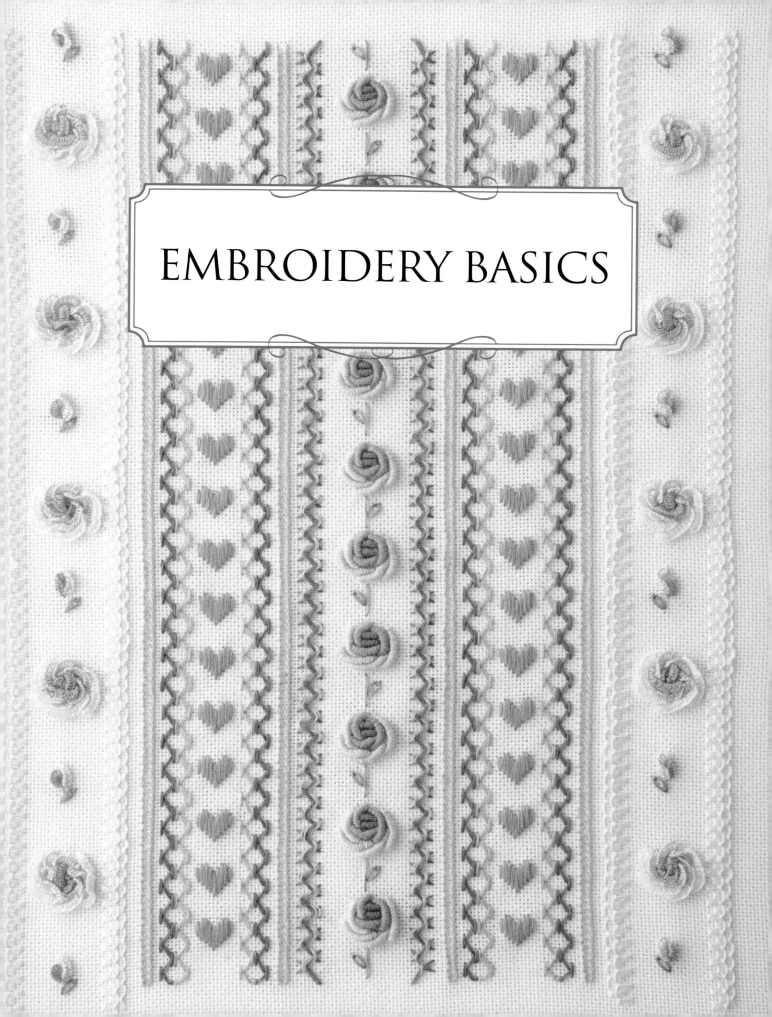

EMBROIDERY BASICS

Embroidery Threads

Stranded Cotton 25

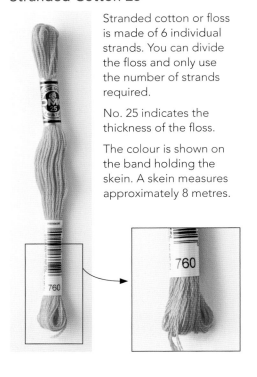

Stranded cotton or floss is made of 6 individual strands. You can divide the floss and only use the number of strands required.

No. 25 indicates the thickness of the floss.

The colour is shown on the band holding the skein. A skein measures approximately 8 metres.

Colour code

The colour code changes from one brand to another.

DMC embroidery thread is used in this book.

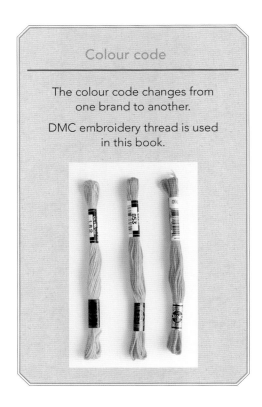

Pearl Cotton 5

Thicker than embroidery cotton 25, this thread is twisted and shiny. The strands are indivisible.

A skein measures approximately 25 metres.

Pearl Cotton 8

This thread is thinner than pearl cotton 5 and is sold in a ball.

Pearl Cotton 12

This thread is thinner than pearl cotton 8.

Other Embroidery Threads

A   B   C   D

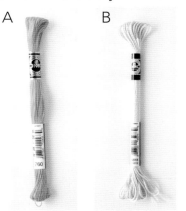

A : Embroidery floss (stranded cotton)
B : Satin embroidery floss
C : Tapestry wool
D : Diamant metalic thread

A. Made of four indivisible strands that are embroidered as one thread. Comes in different sizes, such as No 16, No 20, No 25, etc.
B. Shiny 100% rayon thread.
C. Thick 100% wool thread.
D. Metallic thread.

Pearl Cotton

This thread is twisted and has a silky, satin-like appearance.

There are 4 sizes: 3, 5, 8 and 12. The strands are indivisible. It used as a single thread for embroidery.

Actual Size

1 strand of stranded cotton	1 strand of pearl cotton 8
6 stands of stranded cotton	1 strand of pearl cotton 5

Needles

There are needles to suit each embroidery technique and thickness of the thread.

Sharp Pointed Embroidery Needles

Actual size

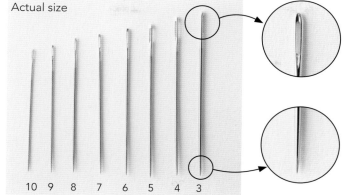

10 9 8 7 6 5 4 3

The larger the number, the finer the needle.

Choose needle size to suit the number of strands of thread used.

The difference between sharp and blunt tipped embroidery needles:

> Not only is the point different, but the eye of the needle is larger than needles with a pointed tip.

Crewel Needle

Actual size

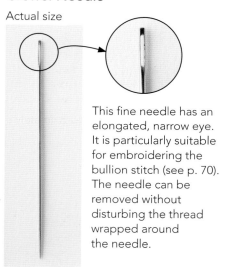

This fine needle has an elongated, narrow eye. It is particularly suitable for embroidering the bullion stitch (see p. 70). The needle can be removed without disturbing the thread wrapped around the needle.

Tapestry Needle*

Actual size

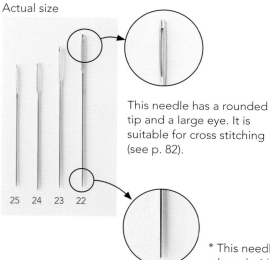

25 24 23 22

This needle has a rounded tip and a large eye. It is suitable for cross stitching (see p. 82).

* This needle is also used to work under a thread without touching the fabric.

Chenille Needle

Actual size

With its large eye and pointed tip, this needle is suitable for embroidering on dense canvas and with thick thread, such as wool or ribbon.

Pointed tipped needles and number of strands

No.10 No. 9	1 strand No 25
No. 8 No. 7	2 strands No 25
No. 6 No. 5	2 to 4 strands n°25, 1 wire n°8
No. 4 No. 3	5 or 6 strands n°25, 1 wire n°5

Blunt tipped needles and number of strands

No.25 No. 24	1 strand No 25
No. 23	2 strands No 25
No. 22	2 to 4 strands No 25

※ The number of the round-ended needle may be different depending on the brand.

Needle Storage

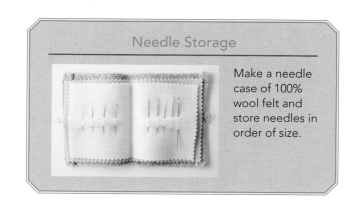

Make a needle case of 100% wool felt and store needles in order of size.

Fabrics

It is possible to embroider on any fabric. However, fabric with a regular weave is recommended. The fabrics below are suitable for traditional embroidery and counted-thread embroidery.

Evenweave, Aida and Zweigart fabrics are the most popular. Linen is also often used for embroidery. See p.82 for the fabric to be used for cross stitch and counted-thread embroidery.

Fabric for traditional embroidery

Off-white linen fabric

White linen

Thread count

The "count" indicates the number of threads per inch (approximately 2.54cm). The larger the number, the denser the fabric.

Fabrics for traditional and counted-thread embroidery

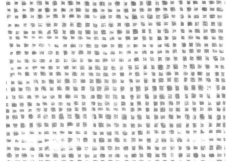

Belfast linen
(25 count)

Cashel linen
(28 count)

Dublin linen
(25 count)

Counted-thread embroidery fabrics

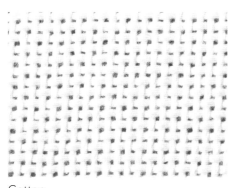

Lugana cotton and viscose
(25 count)

Linen
(20 count)

Cotton
(20 count)

Equipment

Embroidery Hoops

Choose the size according to the item to be embroidered. Hoops with a diameter of 10 cm to 15 cm are practical.

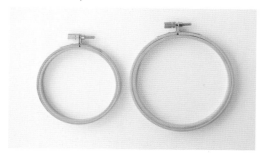

Embroidery Scissors

They are small and have thin, pointed blades.

Embroidery Scissors with Curved Blade

The blades curved to avoid cutting the fabric.

Carbon Paper

Used to transfer the pattern on to the fabric.

Tracing Paper

Placed over the pattern to trace it.

Marker

Used to trace the pattern on to the fabric. Choose a water erasable marker.

Pen

Used to trace the pattern onto tracing paper.

Stylus

Used to transfer the pattern using carbon paper.

Needle Threader

Used to help thread the needle.

Pattern Transfer

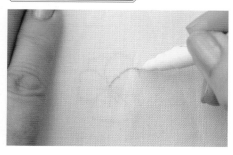

If the fabric is semi-transparent, trace the pattern onto it using a water-erasable fabric marker.

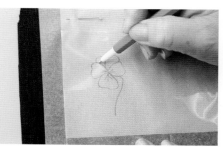

To transfer the pattern onto dark fabric, put carbon paper over the fabric and place the pattern and cellophane on top. Use a stylus to trace the pattern.

Using an Embroidery Hoop

1 Remove the outer hoop. Place the fabric over the inner hoop, positioning the embroidery pattern in the centre of the hoop.

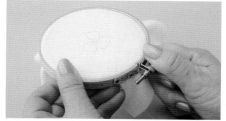

2 Place the outer hoop over the fabric. Then tighten the screw, while pulling the fabric taut.

3 With the fabric taut in the hoop, hold the screw in your left hand while embroidering to prevent the thread from tangling around it.

Thread Preparation
These methods make embroidery thread easier to use.

Stranded Cotton This method gives a thread lengths of 100 cm. It is also possible to take the strands one by one and cut them to the desired length.

1 Remove the labels and set them aside.

2 Separate the floss from the centre to form a loop.

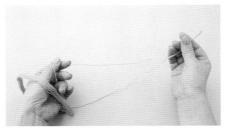

3 Put one hand in the loop. Keep the loop shape as you unwind it.

4 Fold in half the times, then cut at the end. A skein measures approximately 8 metres, so you will obtain 8 lengths of 100cm.

5 Place 1 label over the 8 lengths. Fold in half and place the other label over the ends of the floss.

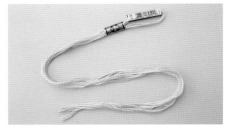

6 Slide the labels to the middle of the skein. All threads have now been cut to the same length.

Pearl Cotton 5

1 Remove labels.

2 Undo the thread and form a loop.

knot

3 Cut the knot from the end.

4 Slip first label over the threads. Fold in half and slide the second label over all the ends.

Pearl Cotton 8 and 12

The end of the thread is found in the centre.

1 Separate the strands one by one from the middle using a needle.

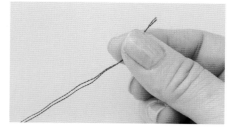

2 Place the required number of strands together.

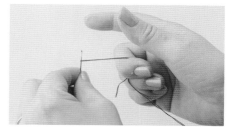

3 Fold the strands and use a needle to sharpen the fold.

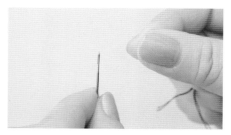

4 Remove the needle from the fold.

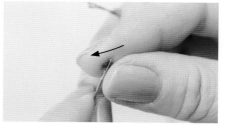

5 Insert the fold through the eye of the needle.

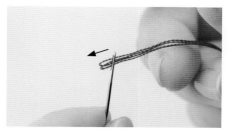

6 Pull the folded strands through the eye to thread the needle.

Using a Needle Threader

To thread a large number of strands or pearl cotton 5, a needle threader is helpful. Insert the tip of the threader through the eye of the needle, then insert the thread in the tip of the needle threader. Pull the tip of needle threader back through the needle.

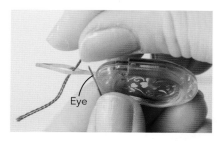

Eye

Thread Length

You can use threads of up to 100cm. If that is too long, cut them in half to obtain a length of about 50cm. Thread the needle and fold the thread back by about a third.

End Knot

Wrap the end of the thread around the needle and hold it with your thumb. Pull the needle up through the thread.

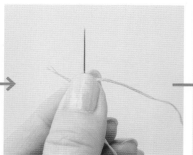

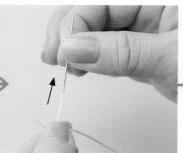

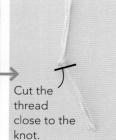

Cut the thread close to the knot.

Starting and Finishing Embroidery

Choose a technique suited the particular style embroidery.

Outline Stitches

Start
On the right side of your work, insert the needle a small distance from the start of the pattern. Bring the needle out at the starting point and start embroidering (1).

Finishing off
Bring the needle out on the wrong side of your work and work it under a few stitches (3).
Work back to the last stitch, working under the stitches, then cut the thread next to the stitch (4 and 5).

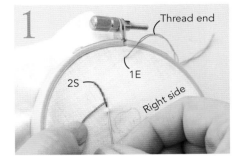

Thread end
2S
1E
Right side

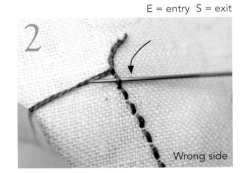

E = entry S = exit
Wrong side

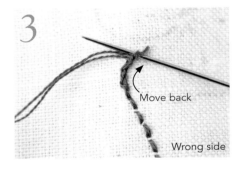

Move back
Wrong side

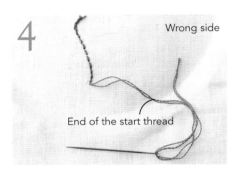

Wrong side
End of the start thread

Wrong side

Filling Stitches

Start
Sew a few stitches in the part to be filled. Cut the end of the thread close to the fabric (1).
Start embroidering the pattern over the first stitches (2).

Finishing off
Bring out the needle on the wrong side of the fabric and work the needle under a few stitches (3).
Work back to the last stitch, working under the other stitches, then cut the thread close to the fabric (4 and 5).

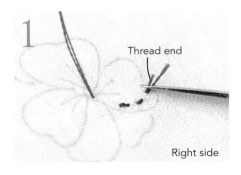

Thread end
Right side

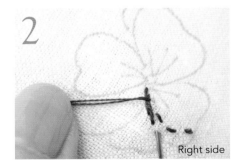

Right side

Wrong side

Run the thread under 1 or two stitches
Wrong side

Wrong side

Knotted Stitches

Start

Sew a cross over 2 threads of the fabric on the wrong side (1 and 2). Bring out the needle on the right side and make the knot (3).

Finish

Bring out the needle on the wrong side and work it under the starting stitch, then cut the thread (4 and 5).

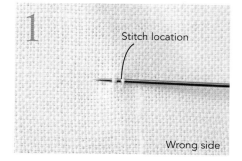

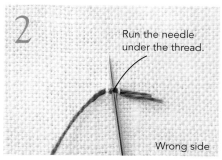

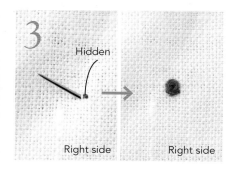

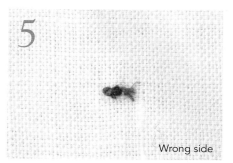

Start of Additional Stitches

If stitches have already been embroidered in the pattern, work the thread under a few of these stitches. Then return to where this thread should start.

Embroidery with Double Thread

Fold the thread in half and insert both ends through the eye of the needle. Work the needle under the embroidered stitches, then through the loop formed by the thread.

Thread the 2 ends of the wire.   Fold

Tips for Obtaining a Neat Finish

1 PATTERN TRANSFER

Iron the fabric, straightening the weave before transferring the pattern. Try to draw the lines of the pattern in one go time to avoid overlapping lines. Follow a straight thread in the weave when drawing straight lines. Using a circle template allows you to obtain precise circles.

Divide the circle equally and put the marks.

Draw a circle using a compass.

2 CORRECT NEEDLE

Choose the size of the needle according to the number of strands. A fine needle is suitable for embroidering with 1 strand. A needle with a sufficiently large eye is recommended for embroidering with more than 2 strands. Choose a large needle to embroider on a thick fabric.

3 REGULAR THREAD TENSION

Take care to obtain a regular thread tension. If the thread is too tight, the fabric may pucker. On the other hand, if the thread is too loose, the stitches may "detach" from the fabric.

4 HOLDING THE THREAD

When embroidering, lightly hold the thread with the thumb of your left hand. This helps regulate the tension of the thread and prevents tangling.

5
When embroidering, the thread tends to twist. Untwist the thread to avoid tangling and sew uniform stitches.

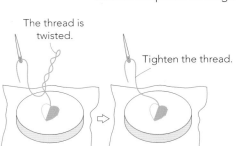

The thread is twisted.

Tighten the thread.

6 PILLING

The thread often pills as a result of friction against the fabric. It is advisable to change the thread if you undo stitches or you notice pilling.

7 SMALL STITCHES IN CURVES

Embroider curves with smaller stitches so that they look as natural as possible.

Embroider with small stitches.

8 WRONG SIDE OF THE FABRIC

It is possible to carry the thread on the wrong side of the fabric to embroider nearby motifs. However, if they are more than 2cm apart, fasten off the thread at the end of each motif.

Wrong side of the fabric

about 2 cm

Fasten off the thread at the end of isolated motif.

Finishing Touches and Care

Finishing Touches

When you have finished your embroidery, check the stitches have been properly fastened off on the wrong side of the fabric. Then erase the fabric marker.

Spray water or dab the pattern with a moisten cotton bud to erase the water erasable marker.
Allow it dry completely, then iron. If the fabric is still wet, the marker lines may reappear and become permanent.

Moistened cotton swab

Erase the drawing

Ironing

Place a towel on the ironing board and iron the item on the wrong side at a temperature suitable for the fabric.

Washing

Hand wash with neutral detergent. Gently squeeze out water and lay fabric flat. Allow to dry in the shade.

LINE STITCHES

Running Stitch

This stitch can create a simple line.
It is also used in the padded satin stitch.

Actual Size

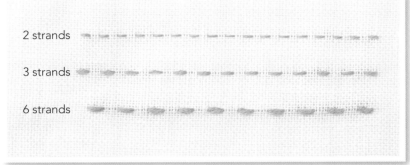

2 strands

3 strands

6 strands

※ Working direction ←

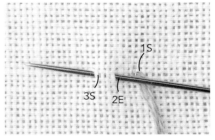

1   Work from right to left. Bring the needle out at 1S, insert at 2E and bring it out at 3S.

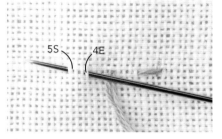

2   Pull the thread. Insert the needle at 4E, then bring it out at 5S.

3   Continue in the same way, making sure you get stitches of a uniform length.

Key points about the running stitch

This is the simplest stitch. It can be combined with the other stitches or used, e.g., with the padded satin stitch to create texture. Insert the needle perpendicular to the fabric. Embroider stitch by stitch to obtain a uniform size. If the thread is too tight, there will be some puckering around the stitches. Otherwise, if the thread is too loose, the stitches may come away from the fabric. It is important that the stitches follow the fabric's surface exactly.

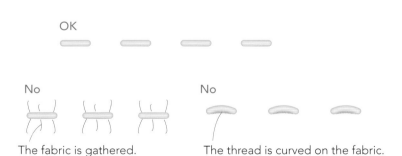

OK

No — The fabric is gathered.

No — The thread is curved on the fabric.

It is also possible to embroider in a different manner. Each technique has its advantages. Chose the best technique for the pattern.

1   Embroider a few running stitches and slide your fingers over them to flatten them. This technique is perfect for embroidering a long line.

2   Bring out the needle on the right side and pull the thread. Insert the needle into the fabric, then pull the thread on the wrong side. This technique allows you to embroider delicate patterns.

Whipped Running Stitch

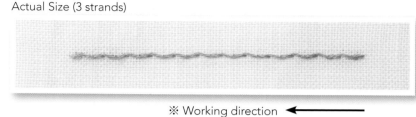

Actual Size (3 strands)

Work a different thread in a downward direction under the running stitches. Depending on the number and colour of the strands, the appearance of this stitch changes.

※ Working direction ←

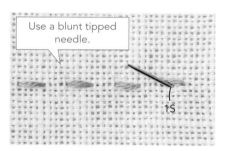

Use a blunt tipped needle.

1S

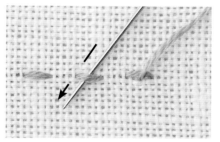

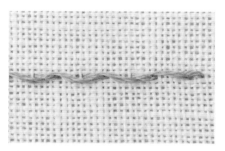

1 Sew a series of running stitches. Pull up a thread of another colour at 1S, under the centre of the first front stitch.

2 Work the needle in a downward direction under each stitch without inserting into the fabric.

3 Continue to embroider in the same way.

Laced Running Stitch

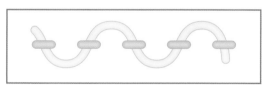

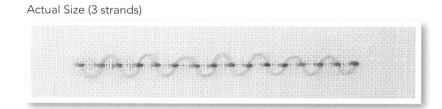

Actual Size (3 strands)

Run a different coloured thread alternately in a downward and upward direction under the running stitches.

※ Working direction ←

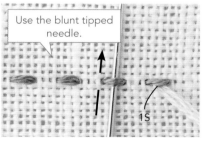

Use the blunt tipped needle.

1S

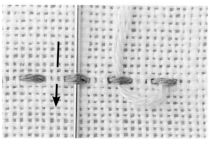

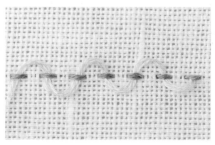

1 Make a series of running stitches. Pull up a different coloured thread at 1S and run it in an upward direction under the next stitch.

2 Pull the thread lightly. Run the thread in a downward direction under the next running stitch.

3 Continue to embroider in the same manner, alternately running the thread upward and downward under the stitches without inserting the needle into the fabric.

Holbein Stitch

This stitch resembles the back stitch. It is worked by sewing the running stitch in both directions to obtain a continuous line. It is also used for blackwork and Assisi embroidery (see p. 125). This stitch is named after the German painter, Hans Holbein.

Actual size (3 strands)

※ Working direction ⟶
⟵ Turn the fabric 180° at the end of each row so that you always embroider from right to left.

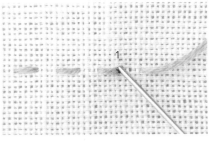

1 Sew a series of running stitches. Rotate the fabric 180° at the end of the row. Insert the needle at 1 (just before the last running stitch).

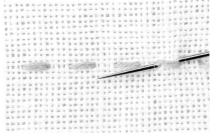

2 Bring out the needle on the other side of the running stitch.

Wrong side

3 Continue to fill the spaces left. Pull the thread to obtain a continuous straight line.

Darning Stitch

Cover an area with running stitch. Turn the fabric 180° at the end of each row so that you are always embroidering from right to left. The length of the stitches on the right and wrong side can be different if required by the pattern.

Actual size (3 strands)

※Working direction
(Turn the fabric 180° at the end of each row so that you are always embroidering from right to left.)

Back Stitch

This stitch can create a continuous line. It is embroidered backwards towards the previous stitch.

Actual size

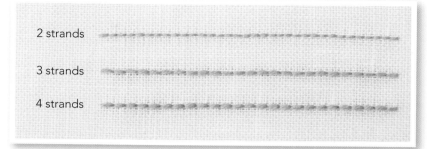

2 strands

3 strands

4 strands

※ Working direction

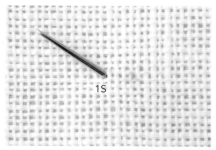

1   Embroider from right to left. Bring out the needle at 1S (1 stitch after pattern begins).

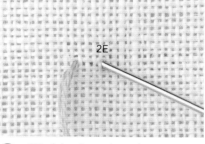

2   Work backwards and insert the needle at 2E (beginning of the pattern).

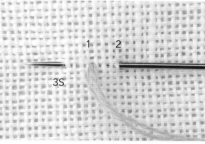

3   Bring out the needle at 3E (2 stitches further on).

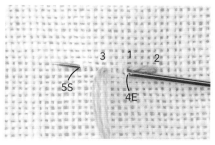

4   Pull the thread. Insert the needle at 4E (same place as 1) and bring it out at 5 (2 stitches further on).

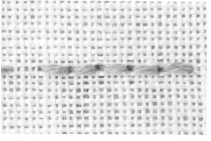

5   Continue to embroider in the same way.

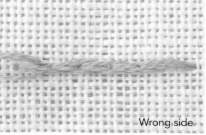

6   View of the wrong side. If the embroidered line is straight, then the thread on the reverse will be split.

Whipped Back Stitch

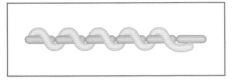

Run the thread in a downward direction under the back stitches.

Actual size (3 strands for the back stitch and 2 strands of contrast colour)

※ Working direction ⟵

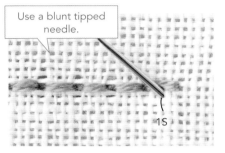

Use a blunt tipped needle.

1S

1 Make a series of back stitches. Bring out the needle at 1S, under the centre of the first back stitch.

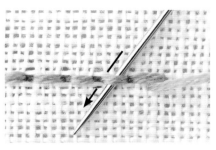

2 Run the needle in a downward direction under the next back stitch.

3 Continue in the same way without inserting the needle into the fabric.

Laced Back Stitch

Run the thread alternately upwards and downwards under the rear stitches.

Actual size (3 strands for the back stitch and 2 strands for the contrast colour)

※ Working direction ⟵

Use a blunt tipped needle.

1S

1 Make a series of back stitches. Bring out the needle at 1S under the centre of the first back stitch and run the needle in an upward direction under the next stitch.

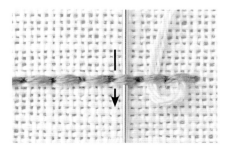

2 Pull the thread lightly. Run the needle in downward direction under the third back stitch.

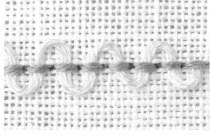

3 Continue to embroider in the same way, alternately running the thread in an upward and downward direction under the stitches without inserting the needle into the fabric.

Pekinese Stitch

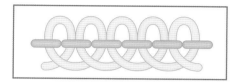

This stitch was often used in ancient Chinese embroidery.

Sew a series of back stitches and work a different coloured thread twice under each stitch.

Actual size (3 strands for the back stitches and 2 strands for the contrast colour)

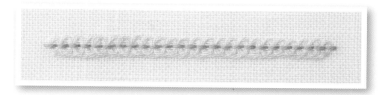

※ Working direction ⟶

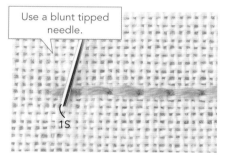

1 Sew a series of back stitches. The Pekinese stitch runs from left to right. Bring out the needle at 1S.

Use a blunt tipped needle.

1S

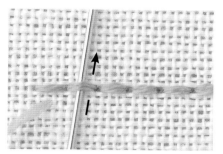

2 Run the needle in an upward direction under the second back stitch, without inserting the needle into the fabric.

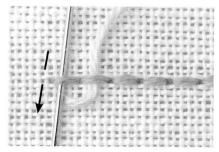

3 Make a loop and run the needle in an upward direction under the first back stitch.

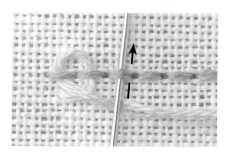

4 Run the needle in an upward direction under the third back stitch.

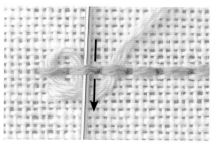

5 Run the needle in a downward direction under the second back stitch.

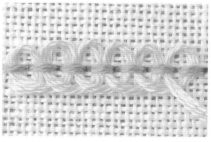

6 Continue to embroider in the same way, ensuring the uniform size of each loop.

Outline Stitch

This stitch can create lines of different widths and allows the creation of intricate curves by using small stitches. Therefore, it is very suited to embroidering letters.

Actual size

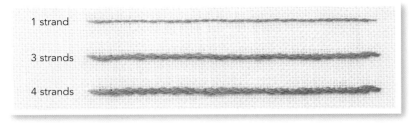

1 strand

3 strands

4 strands

※ Working direction ⟶

Outline stitch in a straight line (*inserting the needle in the same place as the previous stitch.)

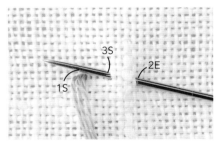

1   Embroider from left to right. Bring out the needle at 1S. Insert it at 2E and bring it out again at 3S.

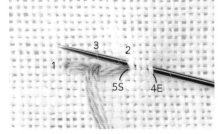

2   Insert the needle at 4E and bring it out at 5S (same place as 2). Pull the thread downwards.

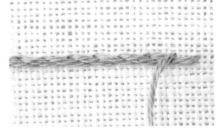

3   Continue to embroider in the same way.

Wrong side

From wrong side, it resembles the back stitch.

Outline stitch creating a thin line

Actual size

Reduce the amount of overlapping for a thin line.

Outline stitch creating a thick line

Actual size

Sew stitches diagonally for a thicker line.

Circle using outline stitch

Turn the fabric as you go so the part to be embroidered is closest to you.

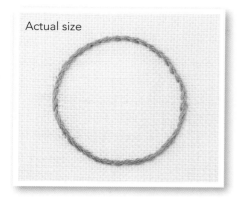

Actual size

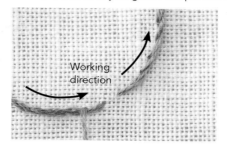

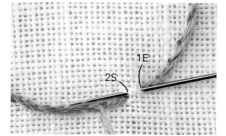

1 At the end of the circle, adjust the length of the stitches to obtain uniform stitches and close the circle.

2 Insert the needle at 1E (the first stitch) and bring it out at 2S.

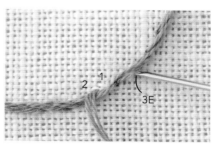

3 Position the thread inside the circle.

4 Insert the needle in 3E (the second stitch).

5 The circle has been completed.

Achieving the same line width at the ends

Actual size

Overlap by a half stitch at the start and end of the line.

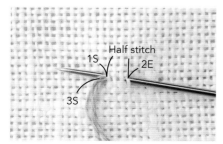

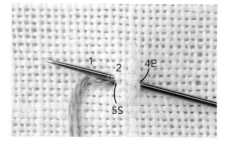

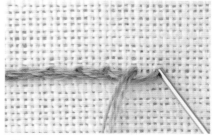

1 Bring out the thread at 1s. Insert the needle at 2E and bring it out at 3S (same hole as 1S). A half outline stitch has been embroidered.

2 Insert the needle at 4E and bring it out at 5S (same hole as 2). The half outline stitch is overlapped by the outline stitch.

3 Embroider the end of the line in the same way.

Embroidering Corners with Outline Stitch

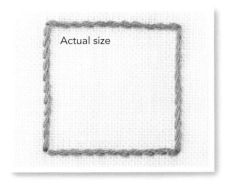

Actual size

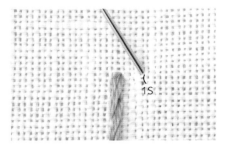

1 Embroider one side of the square using outline stitch. At the beginning and end of the line, embroider half an outline stitch.

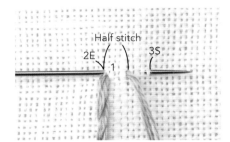

2 Bring out the needle at 1, insert it at 2E (corner) and bring it out at 3 (1 stitch from the corner).

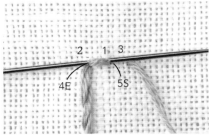

3 Insert the needle at 4E (corner) and bring it out at 5S (same place as 1).

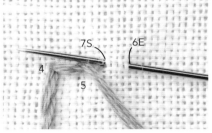

4 Insert the needle at 6E and bring it out at 7S (same place as 3).

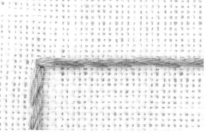

5 Continue to embroider the next side in outline stitch.

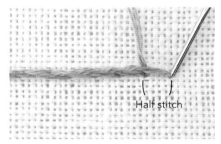

6 At the end of the line, embroider half a stitch over the last stitch. The corner has been completed.

Easy corner

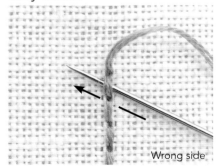

1 Embroider one line in outline stitch, with overlapping half stitches at the ends. Turn the fabric to the wrong side and run the thread under the last stitch.

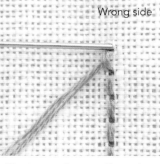

2 Insert the needle in the corner.

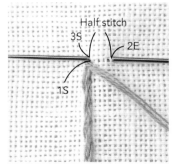

3 Turn the fabric to the right side. Embroider the next line in outline stitch with overlapping half stitches at the ends.

4 The corner is finished.

Outline Filling

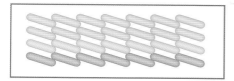

Embroider several rows of outline stitch to fill an area. Turn the fabric 180° to embroider the next row.

Actual size (3 strands)

※ Working direction
(Turn the fabric 180° at the end of each row so that you are always embroidering from left to right.)

Zigzag Stitch

This stitch is a variation of the back stitch. Form zigzags as you go.

Actual size (3 strands)

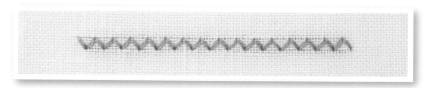

※ Working direction

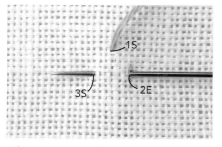

1 Bring out the thread at 1S. Insert the needle at 2E and bring it out at 3S.

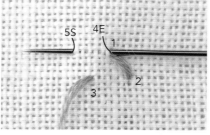

2 Insert the needle at 4E (same place as 1) and bring it out at 5S.

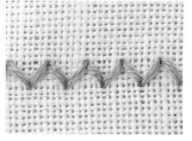

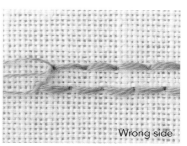

Wrong side

3 Continue to embroider in the same way.

Couching

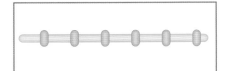

This stitch uses two threads of different sizes. The thicker thread is held in place with the thin thread. It is used to embroider outlines or to fill an area.

Actual size

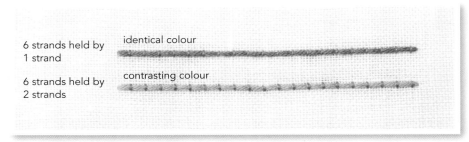

| 6 strands held by 1 strand | identical colour |
| 6 strands held by 2 strands | contrasting colour |

※ Working direction ←

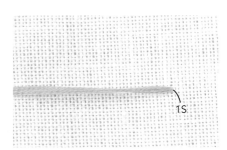

1 Bring out the thicker thread at 1S and lay on the surface of the fabric.

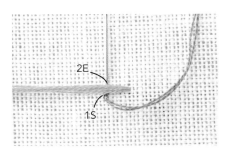

2 Bring out the thinner thread at 1S, below the thicker thread. Then insert the needle at 2E working over the thicker thread.

3 The thicker thread is held in place by one stitch.

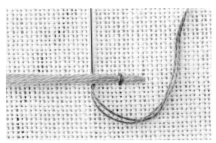

4 Make stitches with the thinner thread at regular intervals.

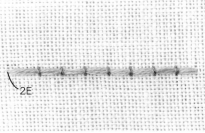

5 At the end of the line, pull the thick thread through to the wrong side of the fabric (2E) and finish off.

Curve

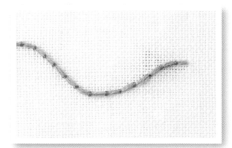

Split Stitch

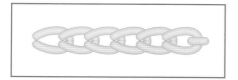

Actual size

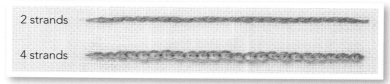

2 strands

4 strands

※ Working direction ⟶

This stitch is worked by pulling the needle through the thread. This stitch can be used to embroider outlines or to fill a surface. It was used to embroider faces in the Middle Ages.

Use two different coloured strands to obtain two-tone stitches reminiscent of the chain stitch.
Embroider by overlapping each stitch by the length of half a stitch, similar to the outline stitch.

Two-coloured split stitch

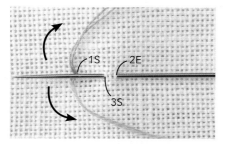

1 Thread the needle with two different coloured strands. Bring out the needle at 1S and position it between strands, separated according to colour.

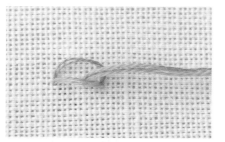

2 Insert the needle at 2 and bring it out at 3. Pull the thread.

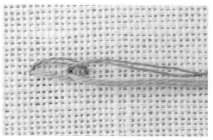

3 Separate the strands according to colour.

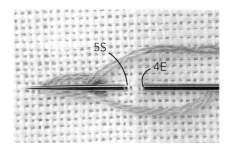

4 Insert the needle at 4E and bring it out at 5S.

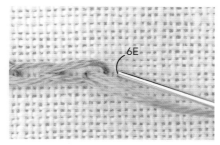

5 Insert the needle at 6E and sew a small stitch to finish off.

6 The two-coloured split stitch has been completed.

Split stitch with a single thread

Work the needle through the thread.

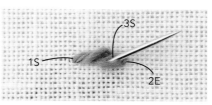

1 Bring out the thread at 1S. Insert the needle at 2E and bring it out at 3S through the middle of the thread.

2 The split stitch with a single thread has been completed.

Chain Stitch

This stitch looks like a chain and can be used to create thick lines.
It is important to embroider stitches of a uniform size.

Actual size

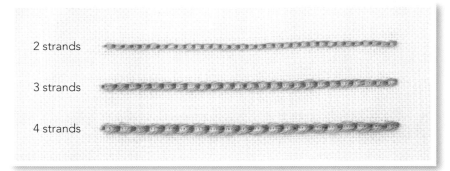

2 strands

3 strands

4 strands

※ Working direction
(embroider vertically)

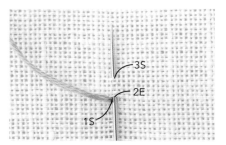

1 Bring out the thread at 1S. Insert the needle in 2E (same place as 1S) and bring it out at 3S.

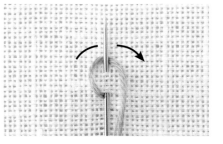

2 Pull the thread from left to right under the needle.

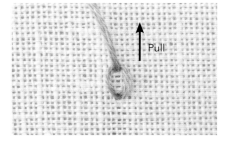

3 Bring out the needle and pull the thread upward.

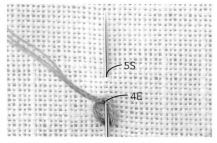

4 Insert the needle at 4E (same place as 3) and take it out at 5S.

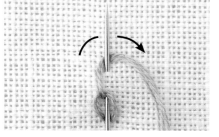

5 Pull the thread from left to right under the needle.

6 Bring out the needle. Do not pull the thread too much in order get stitches of a uniform appearance.

End

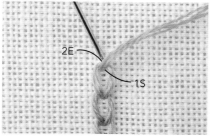

1 Bring the needle out through the inside of the last loop and make a small stitch over the loop to finish off.

2 A vertical line of chain stitch have been completed.

Adding a thread

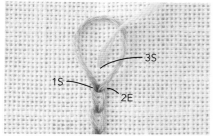

1 On the right side of the fabric form a large loop with the blue thread. Bring out the needle with yellow thread at 3S.

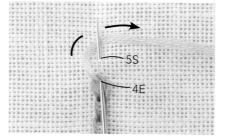

2 Pull the blue thread to adjust the size of the loop. Insert the needle at 4S and bring it out at 5S. Pull the yellow thread under the needle.

3 Continue to embroider with the yellow thread.

Chain stitch circle

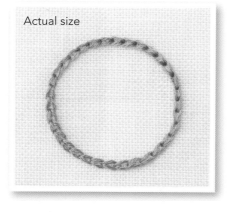

Actual size

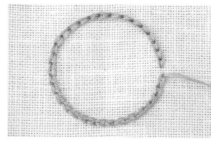

1 At the end of the circle, adjust the size of the stitches to achieve uniform stitches and close the circle.

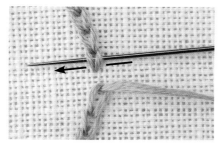

2 One stitch before the start of the circle, run the needle under the loop of the first stitch.

3 Insert the needle into the same place as it was brought out.

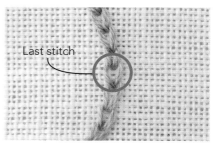

Last stitch

4 The circle has been formed.

Whipped Chain Stitch

Wrap the thread from in a downward direction around the chain stitches.

Actual size (3 strands for chain stitches, 2 strands the contrast colour)

※ Working direction ←

Use a blunt tipped needle.

1 Make a series of chain stitches. Bring out second thread at 1S.

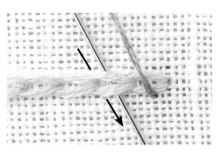

2 Run the needle in a downward direction under the next stitch without inserting it into the fabric.

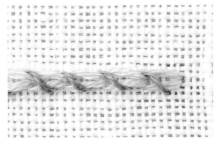

3 Continue in the same way, running the thread under each chain stitch.

Laced Chain Stitch

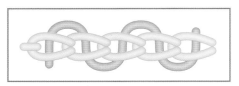

Run the thread alternately upwards and downwards under the chain stitches.

Actual size (3 strands for chain stitches, 2 strands for the contrast colour)

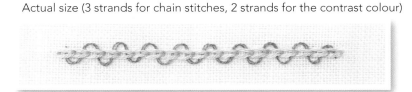

※ Working direction ←

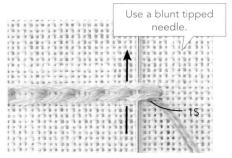

Use a blunt tipped needle.

1 Make a series of chain stitches. Bring out the second thread at 1S and run it in an upward direction under the next stitch.

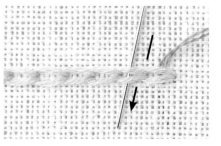

2 Run the thread in a downward direction under the next stitch.

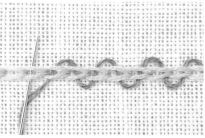

3 Continue to embroider in the same way, alternately running the thread upward and downward under the chain stitches.

Open Chain Stitch

The stitch creates a square chain.

Actual size (3 strands)

※ Working direction (embroider vertically) ←

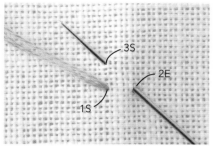

1 Bring out the thread at 1S. Insert the needle at 2E and bring it out at 3S.

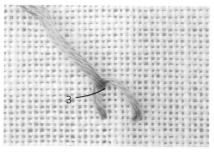

2 Position the thread in the stitch under the needle and bring out the needle at 3.

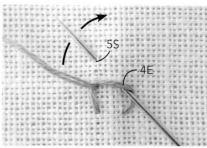

3 Insert the needle at 4E and bring it out at 5S.

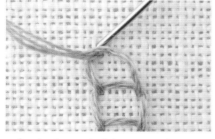

4 At the end of the open chain stitch, make a small stitch to hold the loop on the upper left corner.

5 Bring out the needle inside the loop in the top right corner.

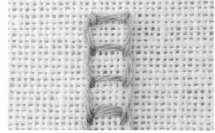

6 Insert the needle just outside the right corner of the loop to create a small holding stitch.

Chain Filling

Chain Filling

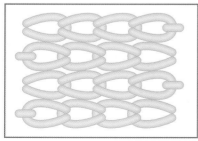

This stitch is used to fill large surface areas.

Actual size (3 strands)

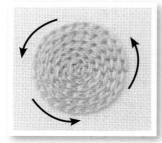

Embroidering from the outward to inwards fill the circle using chain stitch. Embroider horizontally in chain stitch to fill a square.

Cable Chain Stitch

This stitch looks like a chain. Create the loop with a small stitch.

Actual size (3 strands)

※ Working direction (embroider vertically) ←

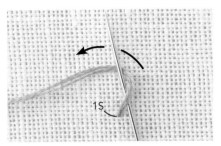

1 Bring out the thread at 1S. Place the needle against the fabric, then pull the thread from right to left under the needle.

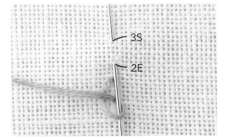

2 Insert the needle at 2E with the thread wrapped around it. Bring it out at 3S.

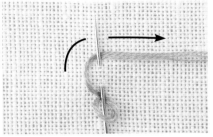

3 Pull the thread from left to right under the needle.

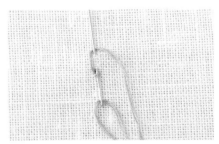

4 Bring out the needle and pull the thread upward.

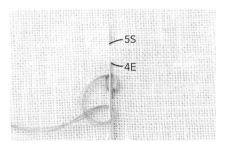

5 Insert the needle at 4E with the thread wrapped around it and take it out at 5S.

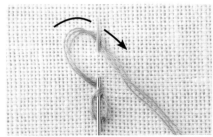

6 Pull the thread from left to right under the needle.

7 Pull the thread upwards.

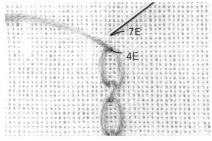

8 At the end of the line, bring out the needle at 4E inside the loop, then insert it at 7E.

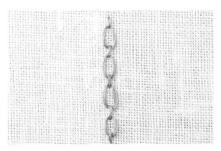

9 The cable chain stitch has been completed.

Twisted Chain Stitch

The chain is twisted.

※ Working direction (embroider vertically) ←

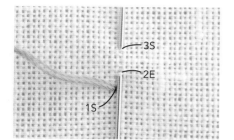

1 Bring out the thread at 1S. Insert the needle at 2E and bring it out at 3S.

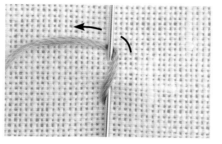

2 Pull the thread from right to left under the needle.

3 Bring out the needle and pull thread upward.

4 Pull the thread upward and adjust the loop size.

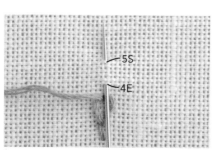

5 Insert the needle at 4E and bring it out at 5S.

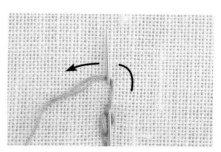

6 Pull the thread from right to left under the needle.

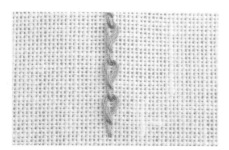

7 Repeat steps 2 to 4.

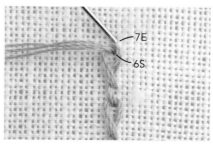

8 To finish the stitch, bring out the needle at 6S and insert it at 7E.

9 The twisted chain stitch has been completed.

Checkered Chain Stitch

The checkered chain stitch is embroidered using two colours. Thread different coloured stands on the needle and use alternately.

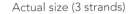
Actual size (3 strands)

※ Working direction (embroider vertically) ⟵

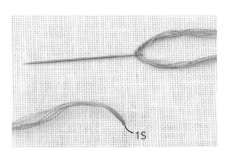

1 Thread two different coloured stands on needle. Bring out needle at 1S.

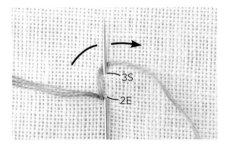

2 Pull one colour under the needle, alternating colour for each stitch. Here: insert the needle at 2E and bring it out at 3S. Pull the blue thread under the needle.

3 Bring out the needle and pull upward.

4 Pull the brown thread through.

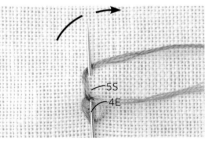

5 Insert the needle at 4E and bring it out at 5. Pull the brown thread under the needle.

6 Bring out the needle and pull upward.

7 Pull all threads upward.

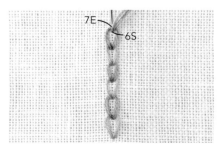

8 Change the colour for each stitch and continue embroidering the chain stitch.

9 To finish off, bring out the needle at 6S and insert at 7E (see step 8) using both colours.

Fly Stitch

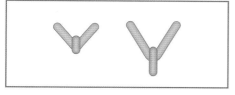

The stitch looks like a fly in flight. The stitch can be embroidered in a straight line, in a circle or in a curve. Several variations are possible.

Actual size (3 strands)

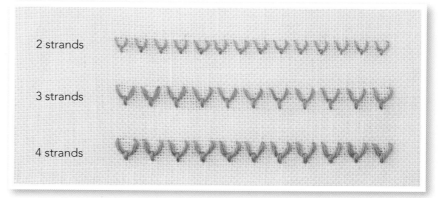

2 strands

3 strands

4 strands

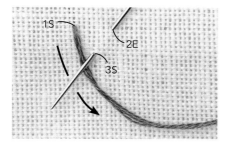

1 Bring out the thread at 1S. Insert the needle at 2E and bring it out at 3S. Pull the thread under the needle.

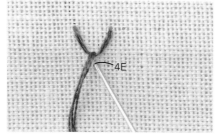

2 Pull the needle and thread downward to form a "V" shape in the thread. Insert the needle at 4E.

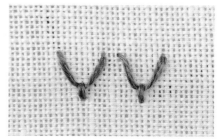

3 Pull the thread.

Continuous Fly Stitch

Actual size (3 strands)

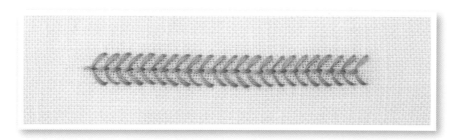

Embroider in downward direction, connecting the small stitches made from 3S to 4E.

※Working direction (embroider vertically) ←

Buttonhole Stitch

This stitch is often used to make buttonholes or decorative edging. It may be embroidered in a straight line or in a curve. It is also used for appliqué, Hardanger embroidery and drawn thread work.

Actual size

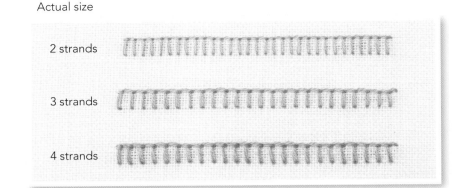

2 strands

3 strands

4 strands

※ Working direction ←

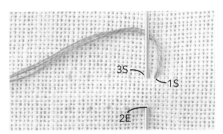

1 Bring out the thread at 1S. Insert the needle at 2E and bring it out at 3.S. Position the thread under the needle.

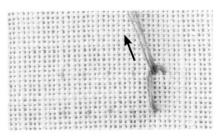

2 Pull the needle and thread upward.

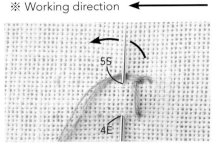

3 Insert the needle at 4E and bring it out at 5S. Position the thread under the needle.

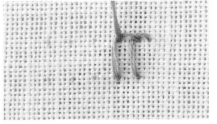

4 Pull the needle and thread upward.

5 To finish off, insert needle next to the last stitch.

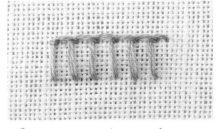

6 Ensure you achieve uniform gaps between the stitches.

Adding a new thread

1 Form a large loop with the blue thread, leaving the end on the wrong side of the fabric. Bring out the new thread (green).

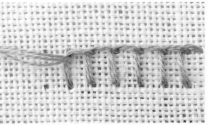

2 Pull the blue thread taught on the wrong side of the fabric to finish the stitch.

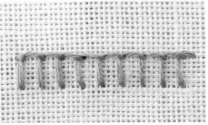

3 Continue to embroider with the green thread. To finish off, slide the needle under the stitches on the wrong side to secure the thread.

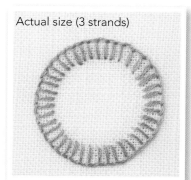

Actual size (3 strands)

Blanket Stitch Circle

Embroider the outline of circle in blanket stitch.

Pay attention to regularity and direction of stitches.

See p.38 the finish of the work.

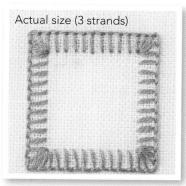

Actual size (3 strands)

Buttonhole Stitch Corners

Embroider the corners of a square with same way that closed buttonhole stitch (see p.40) by inserting the needle several times into the same hole.

Actual size (3 strands)

Reserved Buttonhole Stitch

Embroider from left to right ⟶

Bring the needle from top to bottom, then pass the thread from left to right under the needle. Pull the thread down.

Tailor's Buttonhole Stitch

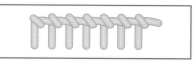

Wrap the thread around the needle to form knots on the horizontal part of the stitch. This stitch is solid and often used as the outline for Hardanger embroidery (see p. 109).

Actual Size (3 strands)

※ Working direction ⟵

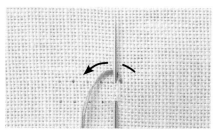

1 Position the thread under the needle as if embroidering the buttonhole stitch.

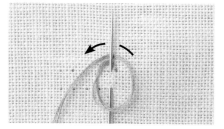

2 Wrap the thread around the needle.

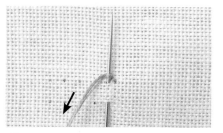

3 Pull the thread tight and slip the needle through it.

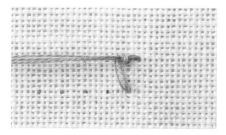

4 A knot forms around the horizontal part of the stitch.

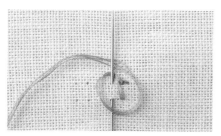

5 Wrap the thread around needle as in step 2.

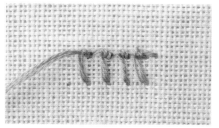

6 Continue to embroider in the same way, ensuring you sew stitches of a uniform size.

Closed Buttonhole Stitch

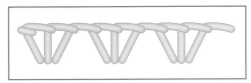

Embroider the closed buttonhole stitch by running the needle several times through the same hole to form the triangular shape. The corners of the square on p. 39 are embroidered with this stitch.

Actual size (3 strands)

※ Working direction ←

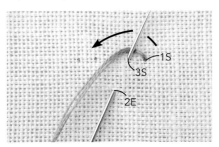

1 Bring out the thread at 1S. Insert the needle at 2E and bring it out at 3S. Position the thread under the needle.

2 Pull the thread.

3 Insert the needle in at 2E and bring it out in at 4S. Position the thread under the needle, then pull the needle upward.

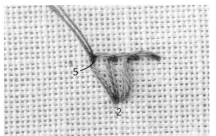

4 Insert the needle at 2 and bring it out at 5. Position the thread under the needle, then pull the needle up.

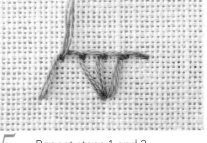

5 Repeat steps 1 and 2.

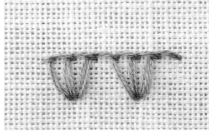

6 Repeat steps 2 to 4. Two closed buttonhole stitches have embroidered.

Closed Buttonhole Stitch

Horizontal stitches overlap yhe contour of the motif. This allows you to cut the outline of the motif without fraying. This stitch is also used for Richelieu embroidery (see p.125)

Actual size (3 strands)

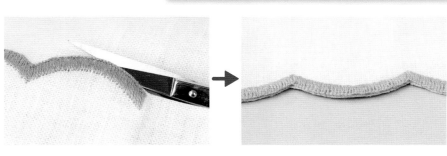

Embroider the outline of the motif in closed buttonhole stitch, then cut the fabric flush with the stitches.

Double Buttonhole Stitch

Actual size (3 strands)

Embroider a row of buttonhole stitch, then turn the fabric 180° so the fabric is now upside down. Embroider the next row in-between the stitches of the first row.

※ Working direction (turn the fabric 180° at the end of the first row)

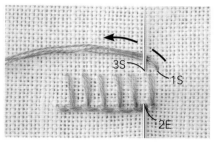

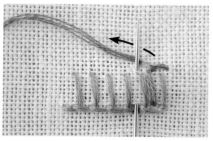

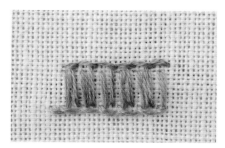

1 Embroider a row of buttonhole stitch. Turn the fabric 180°. Bring out the thread at 1S. Insert the needle at 2E and take it out at 3S.

2 Position the thread under the needle. Bring out the needle and pull the thread up. Continue to embroider in the same way.

3 Embroider a small stitch to finish off.

Buttonhole Wheel

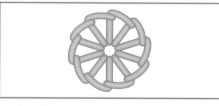

Actual size (3 strands)

Embroider a circle with buttonhole stitch. This stitch is often used to represent a flower.

1 Embroider a circle of the buttonhole stitches by always inserting the needle in the centre of the circle. To finish off, place the needle under the first stitch from the outside of the circle.

2 Pull the thread under the stitch to the inside of the circle.

3 Insert the needle in the centre of the circle.

Up and Down Buttonhole Stitch

Each stitch appears to be double embroidered. The horizontal thread between the stitches is slightly loose.

Actual size (3 strands)

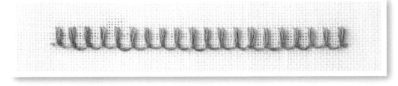

※ Working direction ⟶

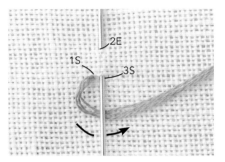

1 Bring out the thread at 1S. Insert the needle at 2E and bring it out at 3S. Position the thread under the needle.

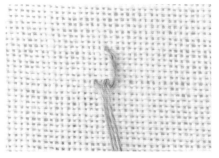

2 Pull the thread lightly. The bottom part of buttonhole stitch is completed.

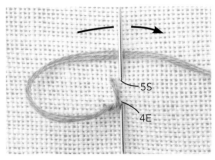

3 Insert the needle at 4E, next to 3S, and bring it out at 5S. Pull the thread from left to right under the needle.

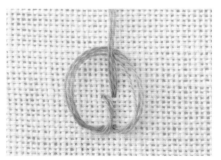

4 Pull the needle and thread upward.

5 Then gently pull them downward.

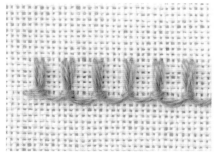

6 Repeat steps 1and 5. Do not pull the thread too tightly.

Buttonhole Stitch and Blanket stitch

These two stitches are similar and the names are often used interchangeably.
The name of the stitch may vary from country to country.

Feather Stitch

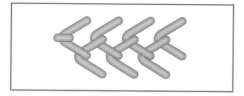

This stitch is often used to decorate the joining edge of appliqué and crazy quilts.

Actual size

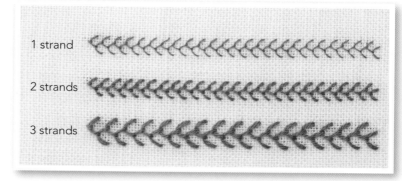

1 strand

2 strands

3 strands

※ Working direction (embroider vertically) ←

※ Draw four parallel lines as reference points.

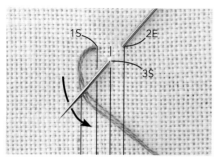

1   Bring out the thread at 1S. Insert the needle at 2E and bring it out at 3S. Pull the thread from left to right under the needle.

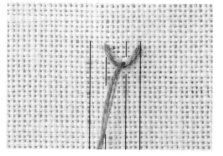

2   Pull the needle downward. The first stitch has been embroidered.

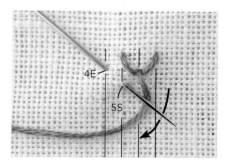

3   Insert the needle at 4E and bring it out at 5S. Pull the thread from right to left under the needle.

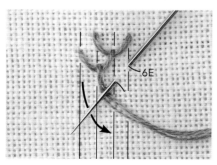

4   Insert the needle at 6E and take it out at 7S. Pull the thread from left to right under the needle.

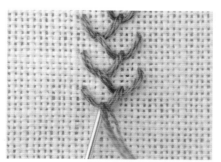

5   Repeat steps 1 and 3. To finish off embroider a small stitch over the thread.

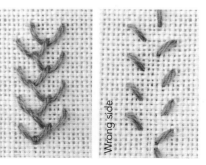

Wrong side

6   The feather stitch has been completed.

Double Feather Stitch

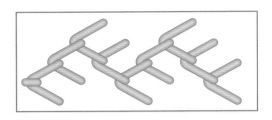

Embroider two feather stitches alternately to the left and the right.

Actual size (3 strands)

※ Working direction (embroider vertically) ⟵

※ Draw five parallel lines as reference points.

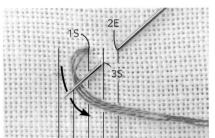

1 Bring out the thread at 1S. Insert the needle at 2E and bring it out at 3S. Pull the thread from left to right under the needle.

2 Pull the needle downward. The first stitch has been embroidered.

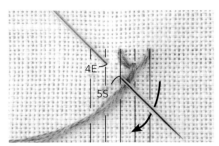

3 Insert the needle at 4E and bring it out at 5S. Pull the thread from right to left under the needle.

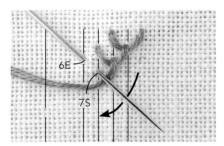

4 Insert the needle at 6E and bring it out at 7E. Pull the thread from right to left under the needle.

5 Two stitches to the left have been embroidered.

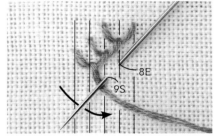

6 Insert the needle at 8E and bring it out at 9S. Pull the thread from left to right under the needle.

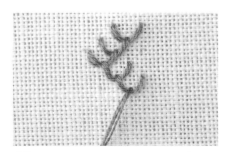

7 Embroider two stitches to the right in this way.

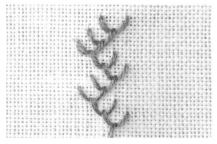

8 Embroider two stitches alternately to the left and right.

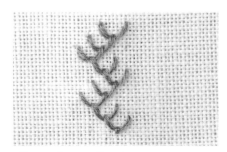

9 To finish off embroider a small stitch over the thread.

Closed Feather Stitch

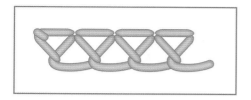

Embroider by bringing the "Vs" of the feather stitch closer together.

Actual size (3 strands)

※ Working direction (embroider vertically)

※ Draw two parallel lines as reference points.

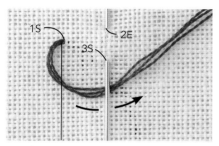

1　Bring out the thread at 1S. Insert the needle at 2E and take it out at 3S. Pull the thread from left to right under the needle.

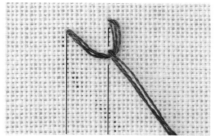

2　Pull the needle downward. The first stitch has been embroidered.

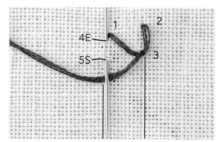

3　Insert the needle at 4E (just next to 1), and bring it out at 5S. Pull the thread from right to left under the needle.

4　Pull the thread through. The second stitch has been embroidered.

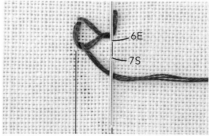

5　Insert the needle at 6E (just next to 3) and bring it out at 7S. Pull the thread from left to right under the needle.

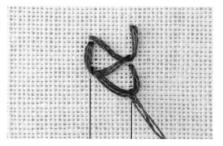

6　The third stitch has been embroidered.

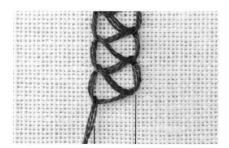

7　Repeat steps 4 to 6.

8　To finish off embroider a small stitch over the thread.

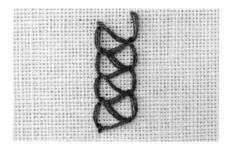

9　The closed feather stitch has been completed.

Single Feather Stitch

Embroider the feather stitch to form a straight edge.

Actual size (3 strands)

※ Working direction (embroider vertically) ⟵

※ Draw two parallel lines as reference points.

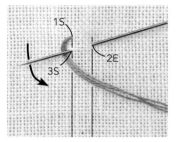 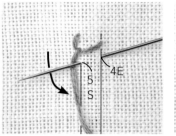  

1 Bring out the thread at 1S. Insert the needle at 2E and bring it out at 3S. Pull the thread from left to right under the needle.

2 Insert the needle at 4E and bring it out at 5S. Pull the thread from left to right under the needle.

3 Embroider the stitches, forming a straight edge. To finish off, embroider a small stitch.

4 The single feather stitch has now been completed.

Cretan Stitch

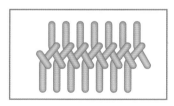

This stitch resembles designs of the Minoan civilization on the island of Crete. It makes a pattern reminiscent of a plait.

Actual size (3 strands)

※ Working direction (embroider vertically) ⟵

※ Draw four parallel lines as reference points.

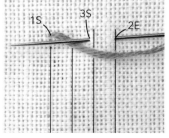 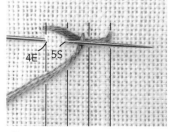  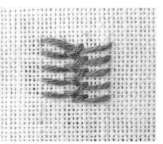

1 Bring out the thread at 1S. Slightly pull the thread downward, insert the needle at 2E and bring out at 3S.

2 Pull the thread slightly downward. Insert the needle at 4E and bring it out at 5S.

3 Repeat steps 1 and 2. To finish off, make a small stitch in the centre.

4 The Cretan stitch has been completed.

Open Cretan Stitch

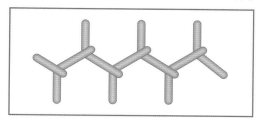

This stitch is often used to embroider a wide line.

Actual size (3 strands)

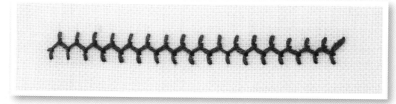

※ Working direction (embroider vertically)

※ Draw four parallel lines as reference points.

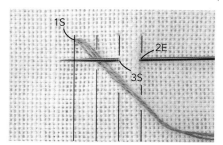

1 Bring up the thread at 1S and pull it slightly downward. Insert the needle at 2E and bring it out at 3S.

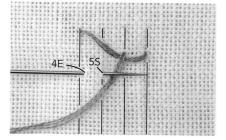

2 Pull the thread slightly downward. Insert the needle at 4E and bring it out at 5S.

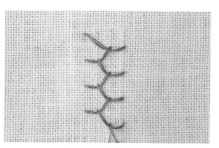

3 Repeat steps 1 and 2. To finish off, make a small stitch in the centre.

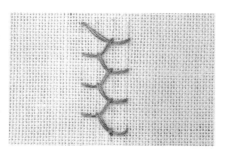

4 The open Cretan stitch has been completed.

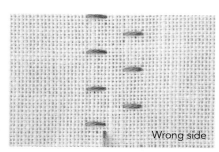

5 View of the wrong side

Cretan stitch embroidered leaf

※ Working direction

Herringbone Stitch

Embroider from left to right crossing threads to create a chevron pattern.

Actual size   ※ Working direction ➡

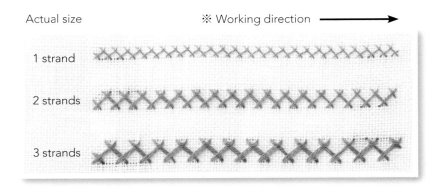

1 strand

2 strands

3 strands

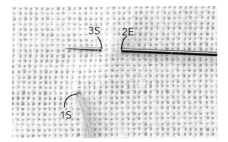

1 Bring out the thread at 1S. Insert the needle at 2E and take it out at 3S.

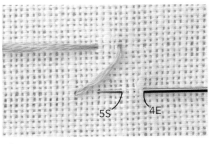

2 Insert the needle at 4E and bring it out at 5S.

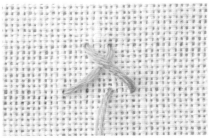

3 Pull the thread through.

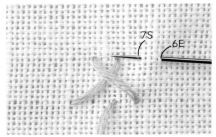

4 Insert the needle at 6S and bring it out at 7S.

5 Pull the thread though.

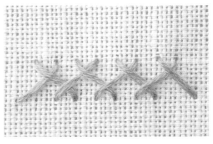

6 Repeat steps 1 to 5.

Shadow Work

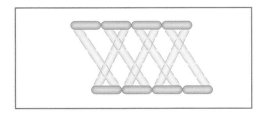

Embroider closed herringbone stitches on the wrong side of fine fabric so that the threads show through on the right side.

Embroidered herringbone stitches worked on the wrong side of organdy.

View of the right side.

Closed Herringbone Stitch

Embroider the closed herringbone stitches.

Actual size (3 strands)

※ Working direction ⟶

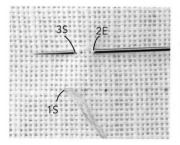

1 Bring out the thread at 1S. Insert the needle at 2E and bring it out at 3S.

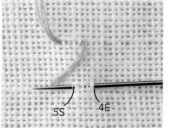

2 Insert the needle at 4E and bring it out at 5S.

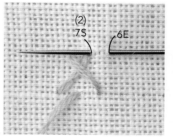

3 Insert the needle at 6E and bring it out at 7S (same place as 2).

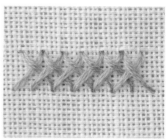

4 Continue to embroider without leaving any gaps between the stitches.

Laced Herringbone Stitch

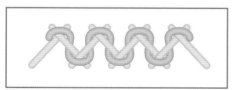

Weave a thread around the crosses of the herringbone stitch.

Actual Size (3 strands for herringbone stitch, 2 strands for the contrast colour)

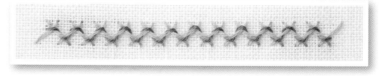

※ Working direction ⟶

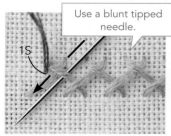

1 Make a series of herringbone stitches. Bring up a different coloured thread at 1S and pull it downward under the cross on herringbone stitch.

Use a blunt tipped needle.

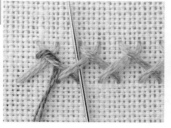

2 Pull the needle upwards under the next cross.

3 To finish off insert the needle to right of the final cross.

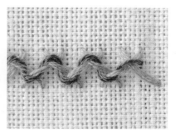

4 The laced herringbone stitch has been completed.

Double Herringbone Stitch

Actual size (3 strands)

Embroider two rows of herringbone stitches by working the second row over and under the first row, filling the gaps.

※ Working direction ⟶

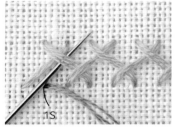

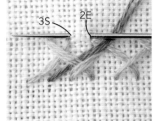

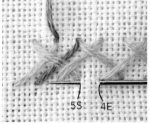

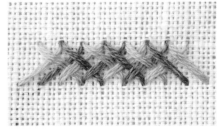

1 Make a series of herringbone stitches. Bring up a different coloured thread at 1S and pull it under the cross in the herringbone stitch.

2 Insert the needle at 2E and bring it out at 3S.

3 Insert the needle at 4E and bring it out at 5S.

4 Continue to embroider in the same way by working over and under herringbone stitches.

Herringbone Ladder Stitch

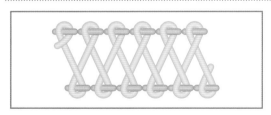

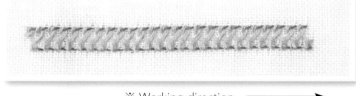

Actual size (3 strands)

Embroider two rows of back stitch, which are offset by a half stitch. Embroider the ladder stitches by working the thread under the back stitches.

※ Working direction ⟶

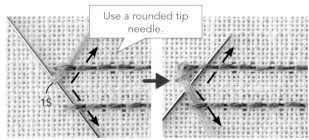

Use a rounded tip needle.

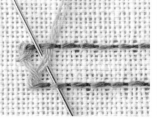

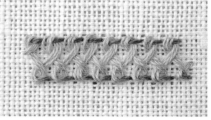

1 Embroider two rows of back stitch. Bring up a different coloured thread at 1S and pull it upward under the back stitch in the top row. Then pull it downward under the back stitch on the bottom row. Embroider the herringbone stitches by working the thread under the back stitches.

2 Pull the thread downward under the diagonal thread and then under the back stitch in the bottom row.

3 Continue to embroider in the same way.

Cable Plait

This stitch is often used to fill an area or to create a wide line.

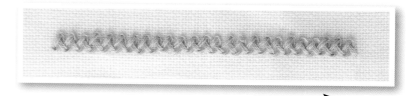

Actual size (3 strands)

※ Working direction (embroider vertically)

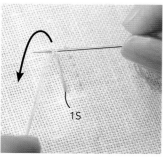

1 Bring the thread out at 1S and wrap over the needle.

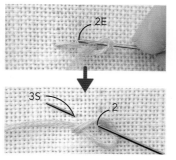

2 Insert the needle at 2E and bring it out at 3S.

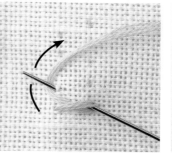

3 Wrap the thread under the needle and bring out the needle.

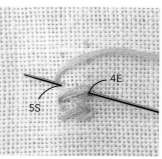

4 Wrap the thread over the needle, insert at 4E and bring it out at 5S. Repeat steps 1 and 3.

Rosette Chain Stitch

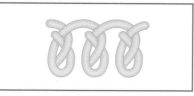

Embroider twisted chain stitches horizontally.

Actual size (3 strands)

※ Working direction

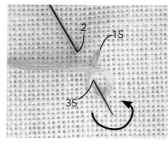

1 Bring out the thread at 1S. Insert the needle at 2 and bring it out at 3S. Wrap the thread under the needle.

2 Pull the thread. Run the needle under the thread at 1.

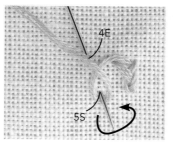

3 Insert the needle at 4E and bring it out at 5S. Wrap the thread under the needle.

4 Repeat steps 2 and 3.

Fishbone Stitch

The appearance of this stitch is reminiscent of fish bones. It is often used to embroider leaves.

Actual size (3 strands)

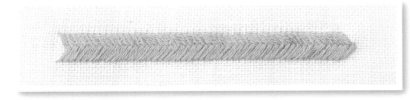

※ Working direction (embroider vertically) ⟶

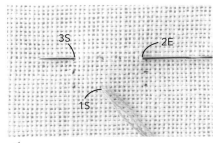

1 Bring out the thread at 1S. Insert the needle at 2E and bring it out at 3S.

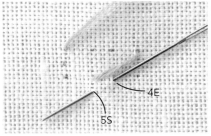

2 Insert the needle at 4E and bring it out at 5S.

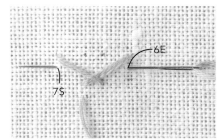

3 The stitches are crossed at the bottom. Insert the needle at 6E and bring it out at 7S.

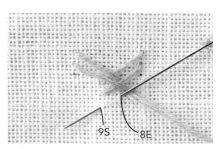

4 Pull the thread. Insert the needle at 8E and bring it out at 9S.

5 Continue to embroider in the same way.

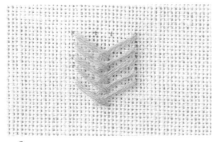

6 The fishbone stitch has been completed.

Leaves Embroidered with Fishbone Stitch

Tight Fishbone Stitch

※ Working direction

Spaced Fishbone Stitch

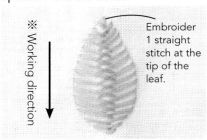

※ Working direction

Embroider 1 straight stitch at the tip of the leaf.

Embroider tightly to fill the surface of a leaf. Embroider spaced to create ribs. Embroider 1 straight stitch at the tip.

Raised Fishbone Stitch

This stitch also looks like fish bones. The stitches overlap more than the previous stitch, creating a 3D effect.

Actual size (3 strands)

※ Working direction (embroider vertically)

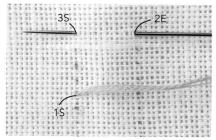

1 Bring out the thread at 1S. Insert the needle at 2E and bring it out at 3S.

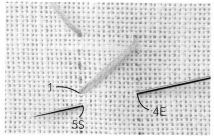

2 Insert the needle at 4E (1 and 4E are parallel) and bring it out at 5S.

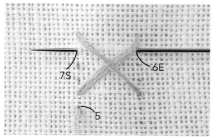

3 A large cross has been formed. Insert the needle at 6E and bring it out at 7S.

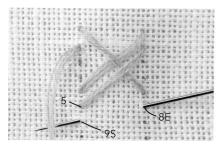

4 Pull the thread. Insert the needle at 8S (5 and 8E are parallel) and bring it out at 9S.

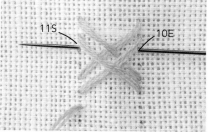

5 Pull the thread. Insert the needle at 10E and bring it out at 11S.

6 Continue to embroider in the same way.

Leaf Stitch

This stitch is used to embroider a leaf. Embroider from the bottom to the top of the leaf.

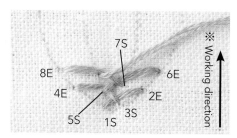

Work the thread from the inside to the outside of the pattern.

Working direction

Chevron Stitch

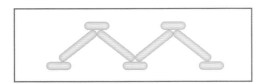

The zigzag is formed horizontally.

Actual size (3 strands)

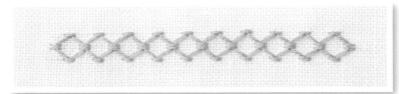

※ Working direction ⟶

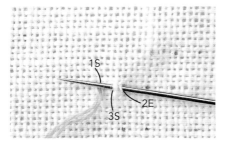

1 Bring out the thread at 1S. Insert the needle at 2E and bring it out at 3S.

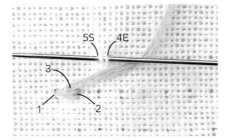

2 Pull the thread. Insert the needle at 4E and bring it out at 5S.

3 Pull the thread.

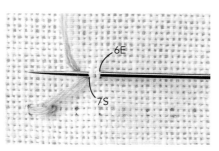

4 Insert the needle at 6E and bring it out at 7S (same place as 4).

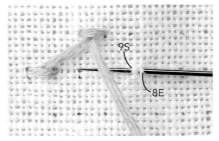

5 Pull the thread. Insert the needle at 8E and bring it out at 9S.

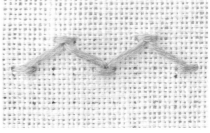

6 The chevron stitch has been completed.

To make multiple rows of chevron stitch

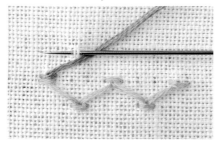

1 The horizontal stitches of the chevron stitches should be parallel in the rows.

2 Two rows of chevron stitches have been embroidered.

> ### Name of the Stitch
>
> The chevron stitch looks like the herringbone stitch.
>
> The difference is the small horizontal line at the end of each stitch.

Vandyke Stitch

The centre of this stitch looks like a plait.

There are two techniques for this stitch: running the thread under the stitch without inserting the needle into the fabric, or inserting the needle in the fabric.

Actual size (3 strands)

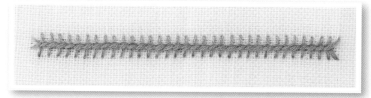

※ Working direction (embroider vertically) ⟶

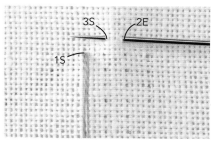

1 Bring out the thread at 1S. Insert the needle at 2E and bring it out at 3S.

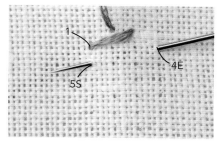

2 Insert the needle at 4E (parallel to 1) and bring it out at 5S.

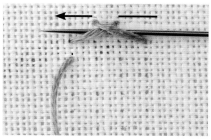

3 Run the needle under where the threads cross.

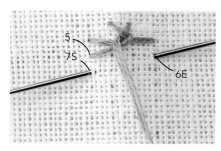

4 Insert the needle at 6E (parallel to 5) and bring it out at 7S.

5 Run the needle under where the threads cross.

6 The Vandyke stitch has been completed.

Inserting the needle in the fabric

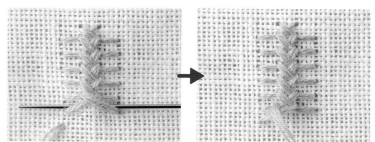

Follow the steps above, but insert the needle into the fabric in steps 3 and 5.

The Vandyke stitch has now been completed.

The Origin Of The Name

This stitch is named after the Dutch painter, Van Dyke.

The Vandyke stitch is used to make smocking and looks like a collar designed by Van Dyke.

However, it is difficult to imagine the collar on an item of clothing embroidered with this stitch.

FILLING STITCHES

Straight Stitch

Actual size

1 strand	
2 strands	
3 strands	

Simply embroider straight stitches. The length and direction of this stitch may vary.

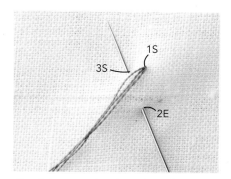

1 Bring out the thread at 1S. Insert the needle at 2E and bring it out at 3S.

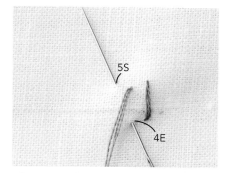

2 Insert the needle at 4E and bring it out at 5S.

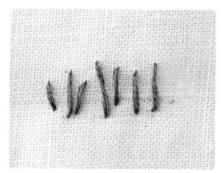

3 Straight stitches are embroidered in downward direction.

Seed Stitch

Actual size (3 strands)

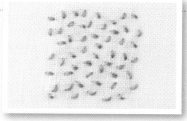

These little stitch are like seeds. Embroider them stitch by stitch like the back stitch. They are embroidered in all directions to fill an area.

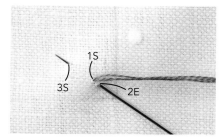

1 Bring out the thread at 1S and insert the needle at 2E to make a small stitch. Bring the needle out at the next stitch (3E).

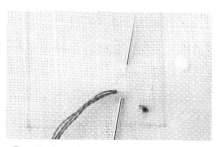

2 Embroider a small back stitch.

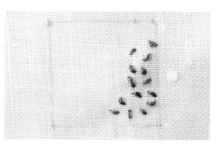

3 Embroider in various directions to fill an area.

Satin Stitch

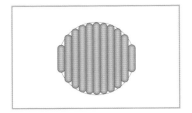

Work the thread from one edge to the other of a shape to fill the entire area.

Actual size

2 strands

3 strands

Embroider from the centre to the edge.

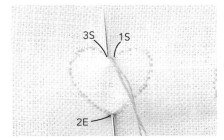

3S   1S

2E

1 Sew a stitch in the middle of the pattern (1S to 2C). Bring out the needle at 3S (next to 1S).

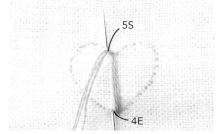

5S

4E

2 Pull the thread lightly. Insert the needle at 4E and bring it out at 5E without leaving any space between the stitches.

3 The left half has been embroidered.

4 Return to the centre and bring out the needle to the right of 1.

5 Embroider the right half.

6 The heart has been embroidered using satin stitch.

Padded Satin Stitch

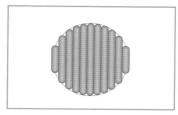

Sew straight stitches, running stitches or chain stitches inside the shape before embroidering it in the satin stitch. This stitch is more 3D than the satin stitch.

Actual size (3 strands)

1 Sew in the inside of the of the shape.

2 Embroider the shape using satin stitch.

3 The heart has been embroidered with padded satin stitch. The stitches underneath are not visible.

Satin Stitch Working Direction   ※ It is possible to embroider both horizontally and vertically.

1 Embroider horizontally from the bottom of the shape.

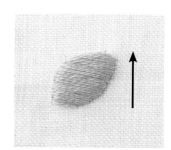

2 Embroider in an upward direction.

1 Embroider from left to right.

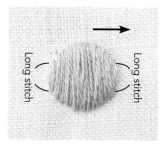

2 To embroider a circle, sew a long stitch at each end.

Long and Short Stitch

This stitch can fill a larger area than the satin stitch. It is alternately embroidered with long and short stitches. This stitch can create a nuanced colour gradient.

Actual size

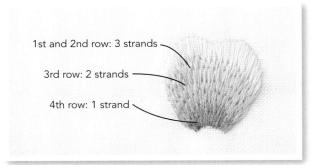

1st and 2nd row: 3 strands
3rd row: 2 strands
4th row: 1 strand

Embroidered pattern over four rows

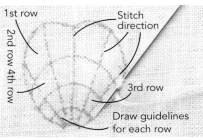

1st row
2nd row 4th row
Stitch direction
3rd row
Draw guidelines for each row

1   Draw guidelines for each row.

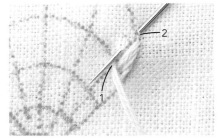

2   Bring the needle out at 1 (inside the guideline) and insert it at 2 (outside the guideline).

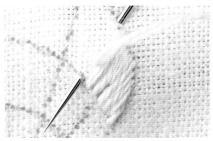

3   Alternately embroider long and short stitches. The length of the short stitch should be approximately two thirds of the long stitch.

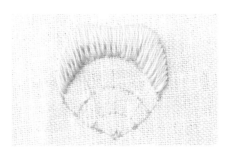

4   The first row has been embroidered.

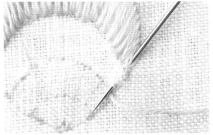

5   Insert the needle at the start of the second row.

6   From the second row, embroider stitches of identical length. By starting each stitch at the bottom of the stitches in the first row (and working in the "gaps" between long stitches), the stitches will appear to be of different lengths.

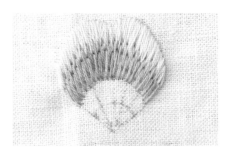

7   The second row has been embroidered.

8   Embroider the third row in the same way as the second row using two strands. Embroider the fourth row using one strand.

With an Embroidered Outline

Embroider the outline with outline stitch or split stitch to enhance the satin stitch.

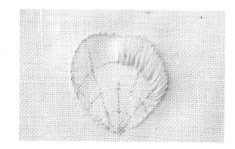

Second Row

Several techniques can be used to embroider the second row.

Overlapping Stitches

To embroider the second row, insert the needle through the stitches on the first row, thus splitting the thread. The colour gradient is natural and allows you to embroider complex patterns.

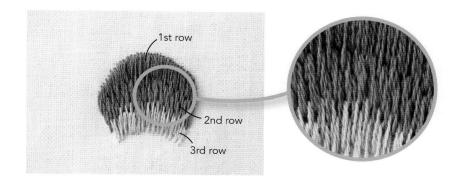

1st row
2nd row
3rd row

Between Stitches

To embroider the second row, insert the needle between the stitches of the first row. This type of embroidery provides good coverage and allows a smooth finish.

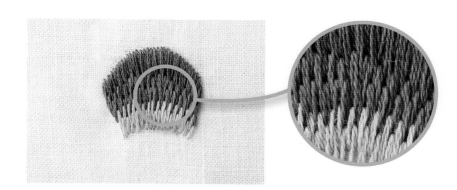

Stitches Positioned End to End

To embroider the second row, insert the needle at the bottom of the stitches on the first row. This technique defines the outline of the rows.

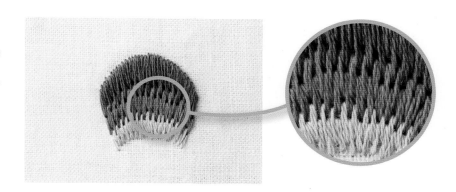

Lazy Daisy Stitch

This stitch is often used to embroider petals. Work in a circle to create a flower shape.

Actual size

2 strands   3 strands   4 strands

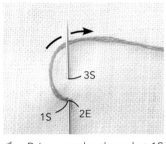

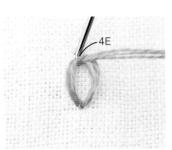

1 Bring out the thread at 1S and insert the needle at 2E. Bring the need out at 3S and wrap the thread under the needle.

2 Pull the thread up and adjust the loop size.

3 Insert the needle at 4E, outside the loop.

4 The lazy daisy stitch has now been completed.

Double Lazy Daisy Stitch

Embroider a lazy daisy stitch inside another lazy daisy stitch.

Actual size (outside stitch: 3 strands, inside stitch: 2 strands)

1 Embroider a series of lazy daisy stitches. Bring out the needle inside the loop.

2 Insert the needle inside the loop and wrap the thread under the needle.

3 Pull the thread to form a small loop.

4 Insert the needle outside the loop that has just been formed. A double lazy daisy stitch has been embroidered.

Tulip Stitch

Run the thread under the vertical stitch to form the loop. This stitch creates a flower reminiscent of the tulip.

Actual size (3 strands)

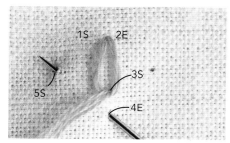

1 Bring out the thread at 1S and insert the needle at 2E. Bring out the needle at 3S, insert it at 4E and bring it out at 5S.

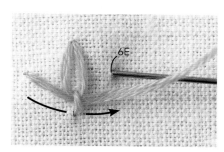

2 Run the thread under the small vertical stitch and insert the needle at 6E.

3 The tulip stitch has been completed.

Ring Stitch

Form a loop with the thread and hold it place with a small stitch. The loop lifts up from the fabric.

Actual size (3 strands)

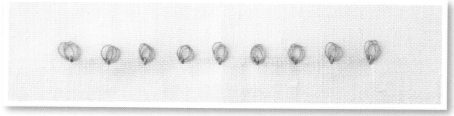

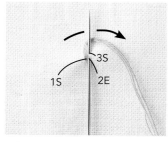

1 Bring out the needle at 1S, insert it at 2E and bring it out at 3S. Pull the thread under the needle.

2 Bring out the needle.

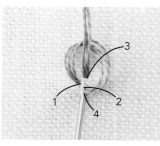

3 Pull the thread to form a loop. Insert the needle at 4 (under 3).

4 A small stitch holds the loop.

French Knot

This stitch forms a small knot.
The knot size depends the number of strands and wraps.

Actual size (the thread has been wrapped twice times around the needle)

2 strands										
3 strands										
4 strands										

Thread wrapped twice

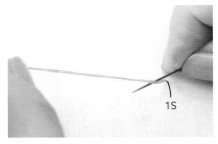

1 Bring out the thread at 1S. Hold it with your left hand.

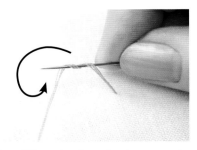

2 Wrap the thread twice around the needle.

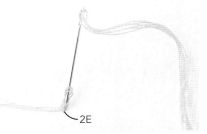

3 Insert the needle at 2E (on top of 1) to secure the knot.

Wrong side

4 View of the wrong side. Pass the needle between your fingers.

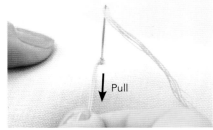

Pull

5 On the right side of the fabric, pull the thread down towards the fabric to bring the knot closer to the fabric.

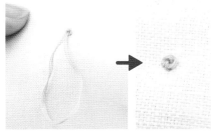

6 Pull the needle through while holding the fabric with your left hand. A French knot has been embroidered.

Thread Loosely Wrapped Twice

Actual size

3 strands

Thread Wrapped Once

Actual size

3 strands

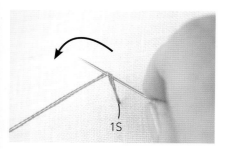

1S

1 Bring out the thread at 1S. Hold it with your left hand. Wrap the thread once around the needle.

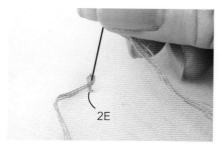

2E

2 Insert the needle at 2E (on top of 1).

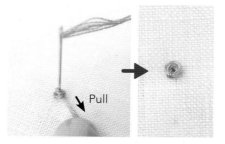

Pull

3 Pull the thread to form the knot. Remove the needle.

French Knot with Tail

Embroider it in the same way as the French knot but insert the needle slightly away from the knot to finish.

Actual size (3 strands)

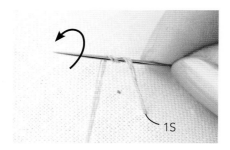

1S

1 Bring out the thread at 1S and wrap it around the needle twice.

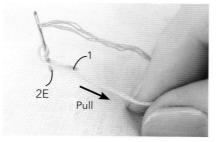

1

2E

Pull

2 Insert the needle slightly away from 1. Pull the thread to form the knot.

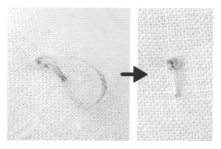

3 On the wrong side bring out the needle and pull the thread.

German Knot

	Square	Triangle
	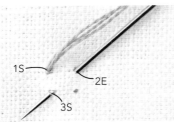	

The German knot is a bigger knot than the French knot. It is possible to make a square or a triangular knot.

Actual size										
2 strands									
3 strands									
4 strands									

Square German Knot

※ Mark four corners for reference.

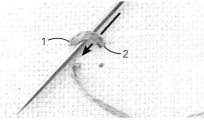
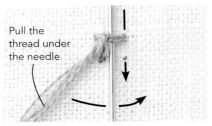

1 Bring out the needle at 1S, insert it at 2E and bring it out at 3S.

2 Pull the thread down. Run the needle in downward direction under the thread between 1 and 2.

3 Pull the thread down. Run the needle in downward direction under the thread between 1 and 2 a second time. Pull the thread from left to right under the needle.

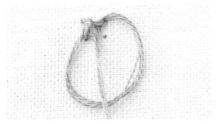
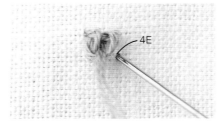

4 Bring out the needle and pull the thread.

5 Insert the needle at 4E.

6 The square German knot has now been completed.

Triangle German knot

Actual size (3 strands)

※ Mark three corners for reference.

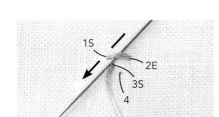
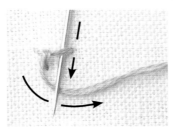
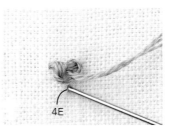

1 Bring out the needle at 1S, insert it at 2E and bring it out at 3E (in the centre between 1 and 4). Run the needle under the thread between 1 and 2.

2 Pull the thread under the needle, then run the needle under the thread between 1 and 2 a second time.

3 Insert the needle at 4E.

4 The triangular German knot has now been completed.

Cable Stitch

Embroider a row of German knots to form a thicker line.

Actual size (3 strands)

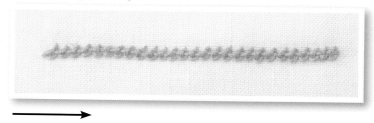

※ Working direction (embroider vertically)

※ Draw two parallel lines for reference.

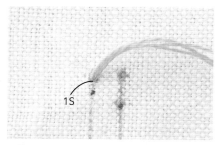

1 Bring out the thread at 1S.

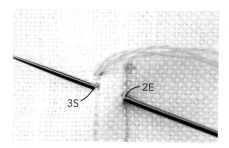

2 Insert the needle at 2S and bring it out at 3E.

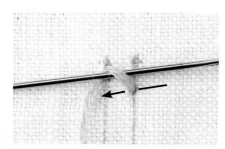

3 Run the needle under the thread between 1 and 2.

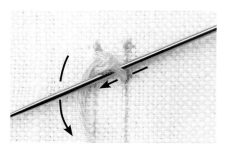

4 Run the needle in downward direction under the thread below 1 and 2.

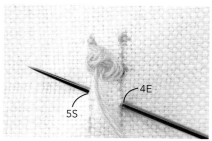

5 Insert the needle at 4E and bring it out at 5S.

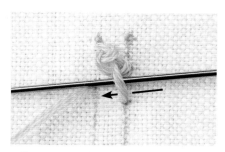

6 Run the needle under the thread between 4 and 5.

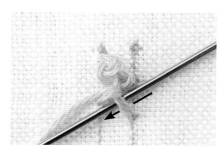

7 Run the needle a second time under the thread between 4 and 5.

8 Repeat steps 5 and 7.

9 Insert the needle at 6E to finish.

Danish Knot

Actual size (3 strands)

This stitch creates a triangular knot.

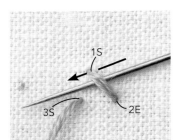

1 Bring out the needle at 1S, insert it at 2E and bring it out at 3S. Run the needle under the thread between 1S and 2E.

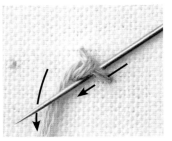

2 Insert the needle again under the same thread. Pull the thread in downward direction under the needle.

3 Pull the thread.

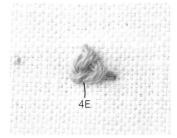

4 Insert the needle at 4E (same place as 3).

Colonial Knot

Actual size (3 strands)

This knot is larger than the French knot.

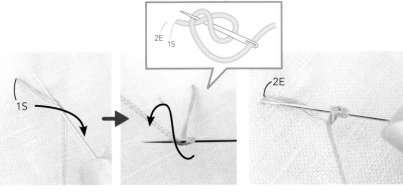

1 Bring out the thread at 1S. Wrap it around the needle forming a figure of "8".

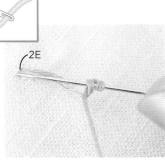

2 Insert he needle at 2E, (just next to 1).

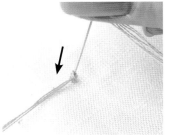

3 Pull the thread and bring out the needle on the wrong side of the fabric.

4 A colonial knot has been embroidered.

Plain Knot

In this stitch three small straight stitches are embroidered to form a pea shape. This stitch is often used to embroider small flowers or the centre of flowers.

Actual size (3 strands)

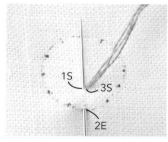

1 Sew a small straight stitch (1S and 3S are in the same place).

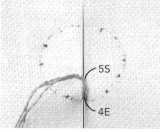

2 Insert the needle in the same place to embroider another stitch right next to it.

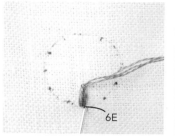

3 Insert the needle in the same place to embroider a third straight stitch.

4 Embroider a series of plain knots to form a circle.

Four-Legged Knot

Actual size (3 strands)

In this stitch a knot is formed in the centre of the cross.

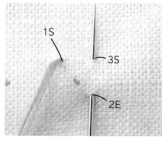

1 Bring out the needle at 1S, insert it at 2E and bring it out at 3S.

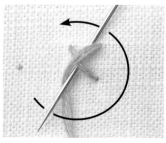

2 Run the needle under the where the threads cross. Pull the thread anti-clockwise under the needle.

3 Pull the thread to form a knot.

4 Insert the needle at 4E.

Bullion Stitch

This stitch makes you think of the golden decoration on a military officer's uniform. It looks like a caterpillar and is sometimes also called "caterpillar stitch".

Actual size

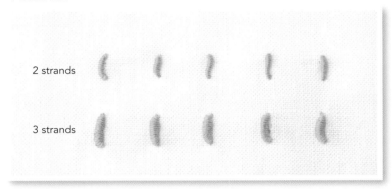

2 strands

3 strands

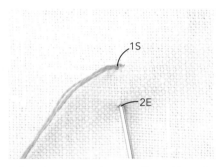

1   Bring out the needle at 1S and insert it at 2E.

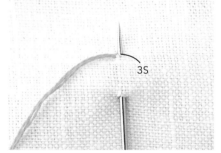

2   Bring out the needle at 3S, just next to 1.

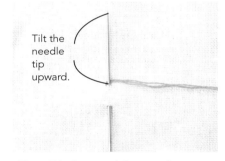

3   Tilt the tip of the needle upward, slightly away from the fabric.

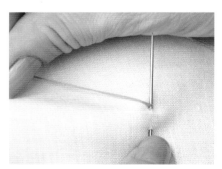

4   Hold the bottom of the needle with your thumb to slightly raise its tip.

5   Wind the thread around the needle in clockwise direction.

6   Push the coiled thread together towards the fabric.

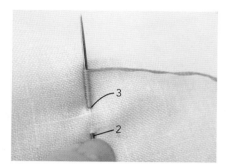

7 The length of the stitch must be greater than the space between 2 and 3.

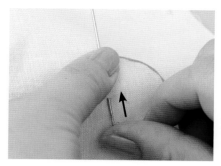

8 Hold the coiled thread with your left hand and push the needle with the thumb of the right hand.

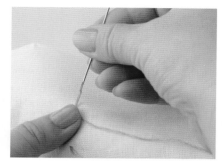

9 Pull the needle through while still holding the coiled thread.

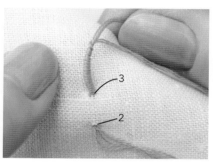

10 The coiled thread is ready to be positioned on the fabric (the thread is not positioned correctly in the photo).

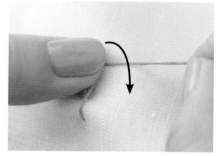

11 Pull the thread and fold the coiled thread towards you.

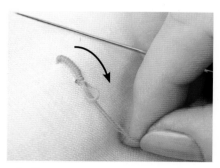

12 Remove your finger and pull the thread tighter.

13 Lightly hold the coiled thread to the fabric and pull the thread towards you to shape it.

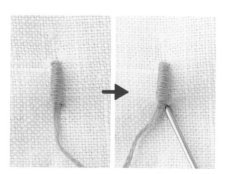

14 Insert the needle at 2.

15 The bullion stitch has now been completed.

Bullion Rose

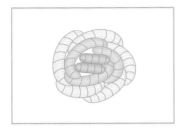

Embroider bullion stitches to create a rose.

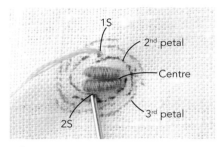

1 Embroider two bullion stitches in the centre of the rose. Take out the needle at 1S (second petal) and insert it at 2S.

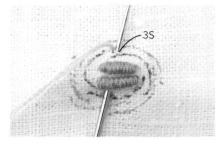

2 Bring out the needle at 3S, next to 1.

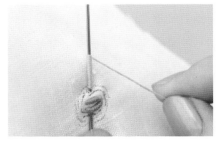

3 Wrap the thread around the needle.

4 Hold the coiled thread and pull the thread.

5 Shape the bullion stitch to follow the outline of the centre stitches.

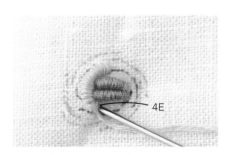

6 Insert the needle at 4E.

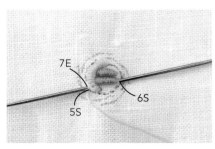

7 Embroider the second stitch of the second petal in the same way. Make the stitches slightly overlap.

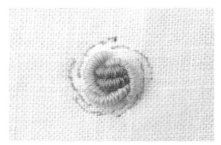

8 The second petal has been embroidered.

9 Embroider the third round in the same way.

Bullion Knot

The needle is brought out and inserted in the same place to form a loop with the bullion stitch.

Actual size (3 strands)

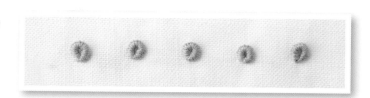

※ Mark the four corners of a square for reference.

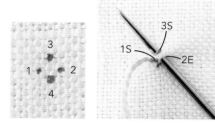

1
Bring the needle out at 1S, insert it at 2S and bring it out at 3S.

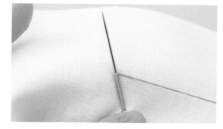

2
Wind the thread around the needle (here it has been wound 20 times).

3
Hold the coiled thread and pull the needle out. Pull the thread.

4
Lightly hold the coiled thread on the fabric with your finger to form a loop.

5
The loop has been formed.

6
Insert the needle in 4E to finish off the stitch.

Bullion Daisy

Embroider a small stitch at the centre of the bullion stitch to hold it in place.

Actual size (3 strands)

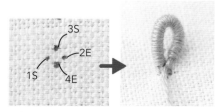

1
Embroider a bullion stitch (here it has been wound 30 times).

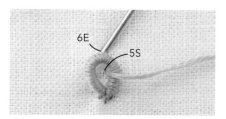

2
Bring out the needle at 5S and insert at 6E to hold in position.

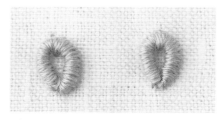

3
The bullion daisy stitch has been completed.

73

Spider Web Rose

Embroider a star with an odd number of legs, then work the thread above / below each leg to make a pattern resembling the spider web.

Actual size (3 strands)

A

B

A : Legs embroidered with straight stitches

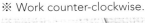
※ Work counter-clockwise.

1 Embroider five straight stitches to form a star.

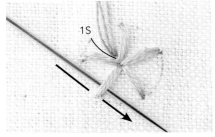

2 Bring out the thread at the centre of the star. Work the needle over, then under each leg.

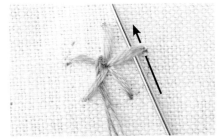

3 The first round has been completed.

4 Continue to wrap the thread around the legs.

5 Continue until the legs are no longer visible. Insert the needle at 2E.

6 The spider web rose has now been completed.

B : Legs embroidered with fly stitch

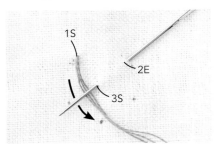

1 Embroider a fly stitch

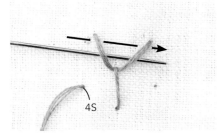

2 Bring out the needle at 4S and pull it under the threads.

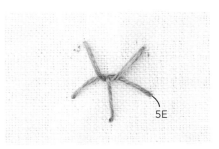

3 The legs have made using the fly stitch.

Ribber Spider Web

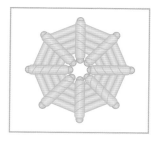

Wrap the thread around each leg.

※ Work counter-clockwise.

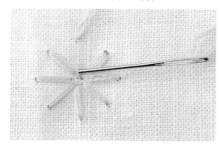

1 Embroider the straight stitches to make a star. Leave a small space in the center of the star.

2 Bring out the needle near the centre.

3 Wrap the thread around one of the legs.

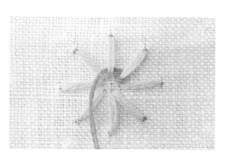

4 Pull the thread close to the center.

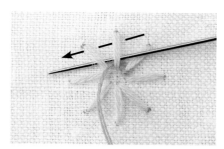

5 Continue to work the thread around the next straight stitch.

6 Do not insert the needle into the fabric.

7 Repeat steps 4 and 5, pulling the thread to form a neat circle.

8 Embroider the second round in the same way.

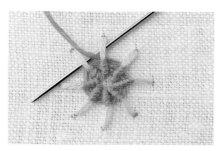

9 Continue to embroider in the same way.

Cast-On Stitch

"Cast-on" refers to the knitting technique. For this stitch loops are formed on the needle and sewn through to create a ruffle.

Actual Size (DMC Special Embroidery Thread 25)

Rose using the cast-on stitch

※ The more times the thread is wrapped, the larger the ruffle.

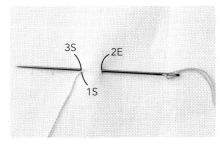

1 Make a stop knot and bring out the needle at 1S. Insert it at 2E and bring it out at 3S (same places as 1s).

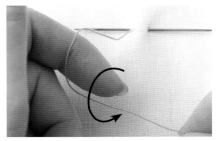

2 Wrap the thread around the index finger on your left hand.

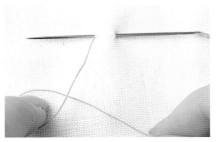

3 Form a loop.

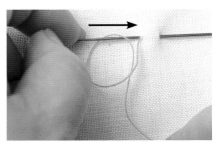

4 Pull the tip of the needle through the loop.

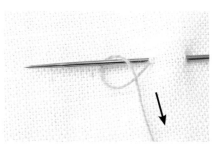

5 Pull the thread downwards with your right hand.

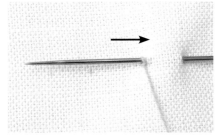

6 Push the loop to the right. The first loop has been made.

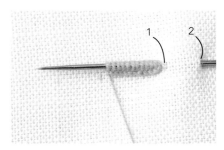

7 Continue to make loops in the same way. The length of the loops combined must be greater than the space between 1 and 2.

8 Hold the loops close to the fabric and remove the needle.

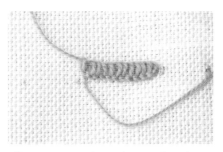

9 Images shows loops after the needle has been removed.

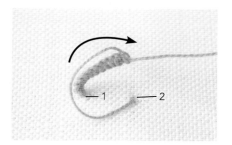

10 Pull the thread to fold the loops back to the initial position (between 1 and 2).

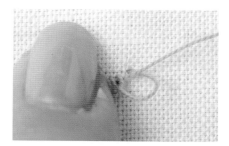

11 Hold the loops on the fabric and pull the thread towards you to shape them.

12 Pull the thread.

Rose using the cast-on stitch

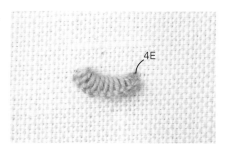

13 Insert the needle in at 4E (same place as 2).

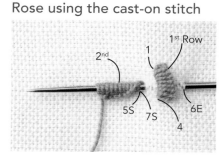

1 Embroider cast-on stitch. Then rotate the fabric 90° to embroider the second cast-on stitch.

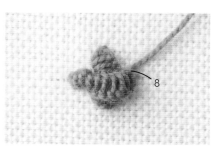

2 Fold the second stitch to the right. The two stitches are crossed. Insert the needle at 8 (same place as 6).

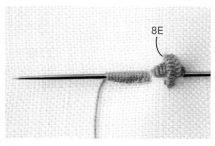

3 Rotate the fabric 90° to embroider the third stitch parallel to the first stitch. The third stitch will be longer than the first stitch.

4 Arrange the third stitch in a curve around the first two stitches.

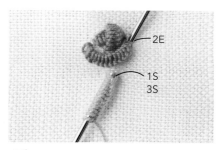

5 Change the thread and embroider the first stitch of the second petal. Turn the fabric so that the needle is parallel to you.

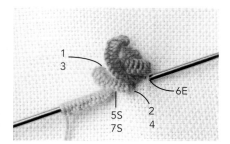

6 Embroider the second stitch of the second round. Make it overlap slightly with the previous stitch.

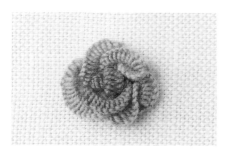

7 Embroider five cast-on stitches for the second round.

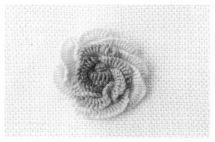

8 Embroider seven cast-on stitches for the third round.

77

Basket Filling

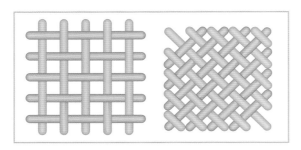

Actual size (3 strands)

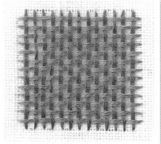

Work the thread above / below each vertical stitch to make a pattern that looks like a weave. The stitch is raised from the fabric.

※ There is a gap between the stitch and the fabric.

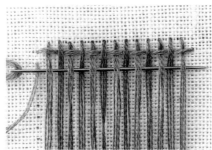

Use a blunt tipped needle.

1S

1 Make a series of long vertical straight stitches. Bring out the thread at 1S and work it above / below each vertical thread.

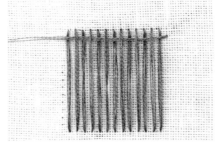

2 Pull the thread.

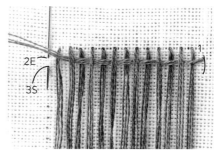

2E
3S

3 Insert the needle at 2E (parallel to 1) and bring it out at 3S.

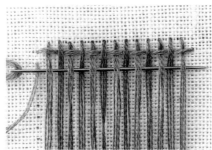

4 Work the thread above / below each thread in the opposite direction to the first row.

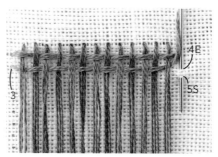

4E
5S

5 Pull the thread. Insert the needle at 4E (same place as 3) and bring it out at 5S.

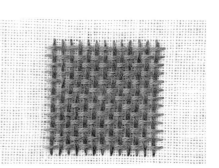

6 Embroider the same way, making sure you get a uniform weave.

Honeycomb Filling

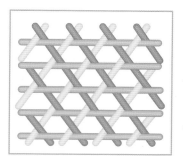

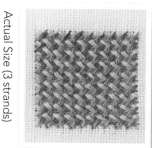

Actual Size (3 strands)

This stitch is a variation of the basket filling stitch. Work two threads diagonally above / below the horizontal threads to obtain hexagonal patterns reminiscent of the honeycomb.

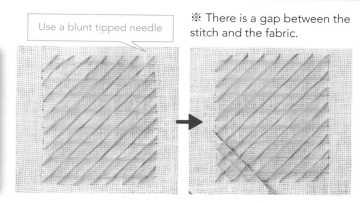

Use a blunt tipped needle

※ There is a gap between the stitch and the fabric.

① Make a series of long horizontal straight stitches.
② Work the thread diagonally above / below each horizontal stitch.
③ Work the thread in the opposite direction above / below each stitch from step 2.

Cloud Filling

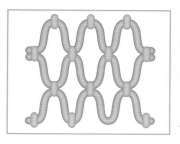

Actual Size (3 strands)

Work the thread in a zigzag under the small straight stitches. Depending on the thread tension, it is possible to make wave or zigzag patterns.

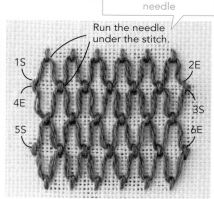

Use a blunt tipped needle

Run the needle under the stitch.

1S   2E
4E   3S
5S   6E

※ Turn fabric upside down at the end of each row.
① Make a series of small straight stitches.
② Work the thread under the straight stitches of the first and second row, forming a zigzag.

Wave Filling

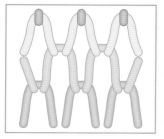

Actual size (3 strands)

This is a repeating stitch that forms patterns that look like waves.

Use a blunt tipped needle

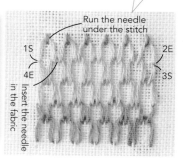

Run the needle under the stitch

1S   2E
4E   3S

Insert the needle in the fabric

※ Turn fabric upside down at the end of each row.

① Make a series of small straight stitches in a horizontal line.

② Work the thread under the first straight stitch of the first row and insert needle lower down on fabric. Repeat until end of row.

③ From the second row, work the thread under the first stitch of the previous row and insert needle lower down on fabric. Repeat until end of row.

Twisted Lattice Filling

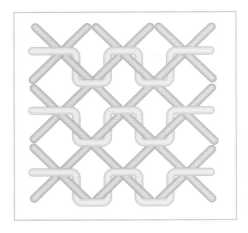

For this stitch make a series of long, diagonal straight stitches in two directions. Then work another thread alternately over and under where they cross.

Actual size (3 strands)

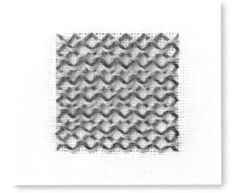

※ There is a gap between the stitch and the fabric.

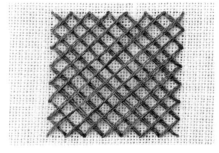

1 Make a series of long, diagonal straight stitches in two directions to form a grid.

Use a blunt tipped needle.

2 Bring out the needle with new thread at 1S and work it over then under the crossing point on the first row.

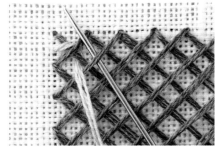

3 Work the needle under then over the crossing point on second row.

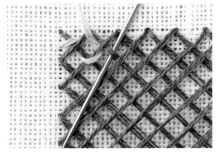

4 Work the thread over then under the crossing point on the first row.

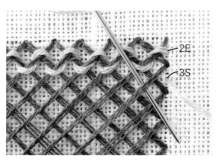

5 On the left end, insert the needle at 2E and bring it out at 3S.

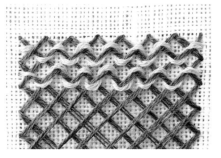

6 Continue to embroider back and forth in the same way.

Trellis Couching

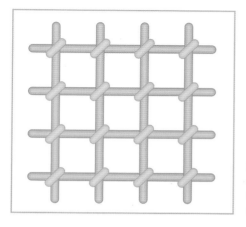

Actual size
(long straight stitches: 3 strands
small stitches: 2 strands)

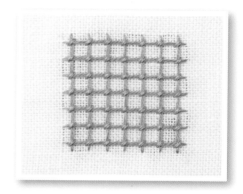

For this stitch make series of vertical and horizontal stitches, then embroider a small stitch where the long stitches cross.

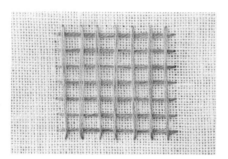

1 Make a series of horizontal and vertical straight stitches to form a trellis.

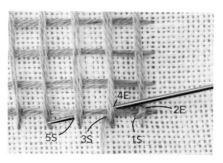

2 Sew a small diagonal stitch at each crossing point.

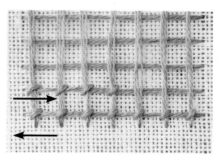

3 Sew back and forth.

Jacobean Couching

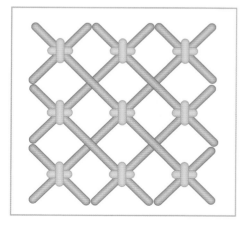

This stitch is a variation of the previous stitch using a series of diagonal straight stitches.

Actual size
(Long straight stitches: 3 strands small stitches: 2 strands)

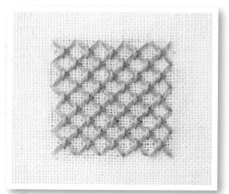

Make series of long, diagonal straight stitches. Embroider a small cross stitch where they cross.

Cross Stitch

This stitch was most likely invented in Central Asia around the fourth century and was further developed in Europe. Count the number of squares in the fabric and embroider by forming a cross.

Actual size

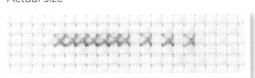

Count

"Count" measures the weave density. It indicates the number of stitches per 1 inch (about 2.54 cm). This measurement is sometimes replaced by the number of threads per centimetre.

The larger the number, the tighter the weaving. Depending on the density of the weaving, the shape size changes.

Actual size

Lugana

Aida (4 pts/cm)

Aida (6 pts/cm)

Fabric

There are special fabrics for cross stitch. The small holes serve as markers for embroidery.

Waste Canvas

Waste canvas allows you to cross stitch on any medium. Pull out each thread individually once the cross stitch has been completed.

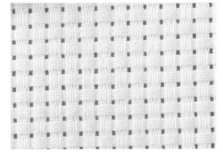

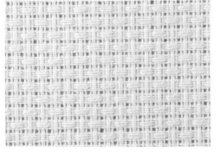

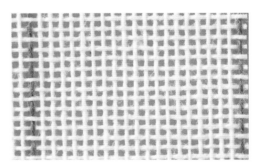

Using waste canvas

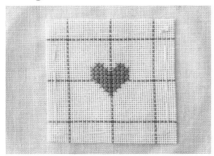

1 Cut the waste canvas so that is larger than the cross stitch pattern. Tack it to the fabric to be embroidered, then embroider the pattern.

2 Remove the tacking. Pull out each thread of the waste canvas individually.

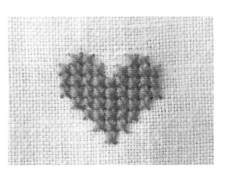

3 The pattern has been embroidered on the fabric behind the waste canvas.

Row of horizontal cross stitch

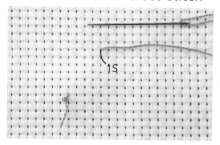

1 Make a stop knot and insert the needle away from the beginning of the pattern. Bring it out at 1S.

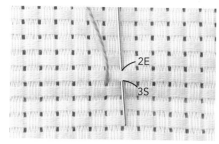

2 Insert the needle at 2E and bring it out at 3S.

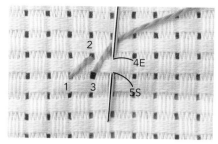

3 Pull the thread. Insert the needle at 4E and bring it out at 5S.

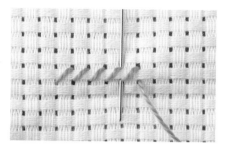

4 Then embroider from right to left to make crosses.

5 The cross stitches have been embroidered horizontally.

Finishing off

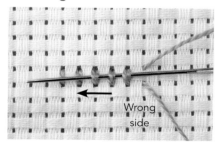

1 Run the thread under a few stitches on the wrong side.

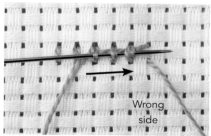

2 Then run the thread under a few stitches in the opposite direction.

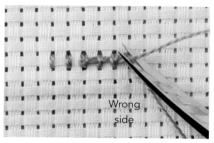

3 Cut the thread.

Finishing off starting thread

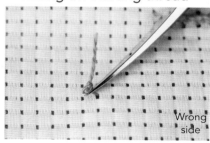

1 Cut the stop knot. Pull the end of the thread to the wrong side of the fabric.

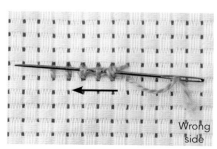

2 Thread the end of the thread through the needle. Run the thread back and forth under a few stitches.

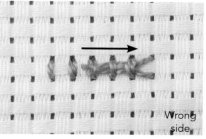

3 Cut the thread.

Working stitch by stitch

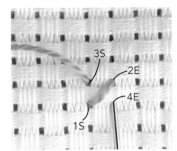 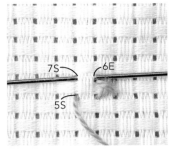 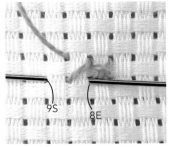 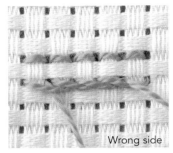

1 Bring out the needle at 1S, insert at 2E and bring it out at 3S. Pull the thread. Insert the needle at 4E.

2 Bring out the needle at 5S, insert it at 6E and bring it out at 7S.

3 Insert the needle at 8E and bring it out at 9S.

4 There will be two parallel lines on the wrong side.

Row of vertical cross stitch

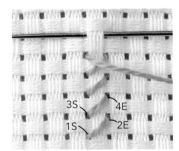   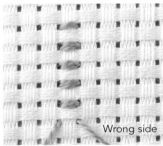

1 Bring out the needle at 1S, insert at 2E and bring it out at 3S. Work half cross stitches in an upward direction.

2 Then work in a downward direction to complete the crosses.

3 The cross stitches have been embroidered vertically.

4 On the wrong side there are small horizontal stitches.

Diagonal row of cross stitch

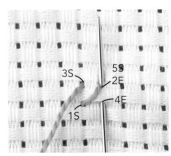 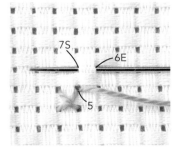  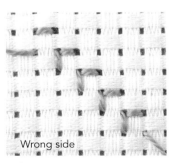

1 Bring out the needle at 1S, insert it at 2E and bring it out at 3S. Insert the needle at 4E and take it out at 5S.

2 Insert the needle at 6E and bring it out at 7S.

3 The cross stitches have been embroidered diagonally.

4 The stitches make corner on the wrong side of the fabric.

Half Cross Stitch

Actual size

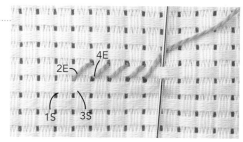

Embroider half of a cross stitch.

Bring out the needle at 1S, insert it at 2E and bring it out at 3S. Continue in this way.

Double Cross Stitch

This stitch is formed by embroidering two cross stitches over each other.

Either cross stitch can go on top.

Actual size

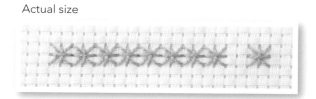

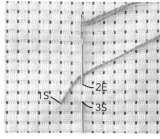
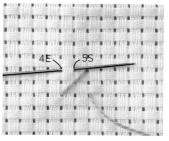
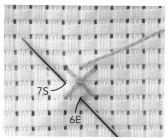
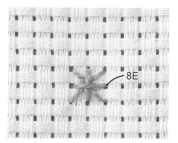

1 Bring out the needle at 1S, insert it at 2E and bring it out at 3S.

2 Insert the needle at 4E and bring it out at 5S. The first cross stitch has been embroidered.

3 Insert the needle at 6E and bring it out at 7S.

4 Insert the needle at 8E. The double cross stitch has now been completed.

Three Quarter Cross Stitch

This stitch is often used to round off a corner.

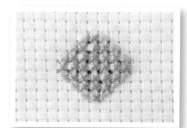

Actual size

Bring out the needle at 1D, insert it at 2E. Then bring it out at 3S and insert it at 4E.

STUMPWORK
THREE DIMENSIONAL EMBROIDERY

STUMPWORK

The origin of the stumpwork is not clearly known, but it is believed it was invented in England in the seventeenth century. Fashionable between 1650 and 1680, this technique was then called "raised work" or "padded work". The most commonly represented motifs were people, flowers, insects and animals, which adorned the frames of mirrors, boxes, book covers or needle holders. A wide variety of patterns was achieved by combining various traditional and raised stitches.

Embroidery was an essential skill for women in this era. They embroidered various objects to show their dexterity. The materials they used are similar to those we use now, such as silk, linen, metallic thread, cotton, etc.

Some older work was stuffed with horsehair instead of wool. In the nineteenth and twentieth centuries, embroidery in relief experienced a new boom and became known as "stumpwork". It is said this name comes from using wood chips for the padding. But it's not certain!

In this technique, we use the "detached stitch" (a detached stitch is equivalent to the simple buttonhole stitch). That means that some stitches are made without stitching into the fabric or by wrapping the embroidery thread around a metal wire. It is also possible to attach embroidered and padded pieces on the fabric.

Stitches and Colours for the Patterns p. 86

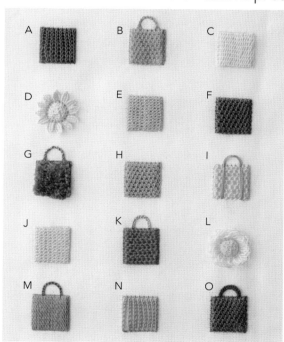

※ DMC pearl cotton 8 has been used for all patterns. The number indicates the colour of the cotton.
※ Insert a piece of felt the same colour as the cotton,

A: Ceylon stitch (3814, p. 96)
B: Corded detached buttonhole stitch (760, p. 88)
Handle: back stitch (p. 21), buttonhole stitch (p 38) working the thread under the back stitches
Pad: straight stitch (D3821, 2 strands, p. 57)
C: Raised stem stitch (445, p. 94)
E: Raised chain stitch (955, p. 95)
F: Corded detached buttonhole stitch (3041, p. 88)
G: Turkey work (840, p. 97)
Handle: Whipped chain stitch (840 for the chain stitch, 2 stands of D3821 for the contrast colour, p. 32)
H: Corded detached buttonhole stitch (352, p. 88)
I: Detached buttonhole stitch (747, p. 91)
Handle: Corded detached buttonhole stitch (519, 3 strands, p. 57)
J: Raised chain stitch (Ecru, p 95)
K: Detached buttonhole stitch (601, p. 91)
Handle: Chain stitch (D3821, 2 strands, p. 30)
M: Raised stem stitch (519, p. 94)
Handle: Chain stitch (840, 2 strands, p. 30)
N: Ceylon stitch (210, p. 96)
O: Corded detached buttonhole stitch (414, p. 88)
Handle: Buttonhole bar (517, 2 strands, p. 90)

Full Size Pattern

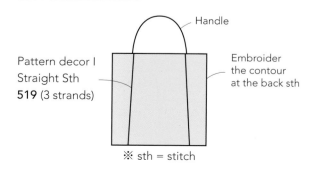

Handle

Pattern decor I
Straight Sth
519 (3 strands)

Embroider the contour at the back sth

※ sth = stitch

※ See p. 92 for patterns D and L.

Corded Detached Buttonhole Stitch

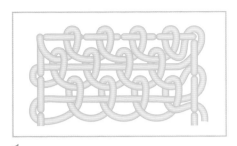

The outline of the shape is embroidered using back stitch. Then embroider the corded detached buttonhole stitches in the same way as the buttonhole stitch.

Actual size

1 Identical Number of Stitches on Each Row

Embroider the outline of the pattern using back stitch. Work the needle under the top back stitch and embroider one buttonhole stitch into each back stitch. At the end of the row, work the needle under the last back stitch at the top so that the needle is outside the pattern. Slide the under the first back stitch on the right side, then pull the thread under the first back stitch on the left side. Run the needle under the buttonhole stitch from the previous row (to the left of the stitch) and under the stretched thread to form the corded detached buttonhole stitch. Make a stitch to the left of the first stitch from the top (1). Do not make stitch to the right of the last stitch from the top (2). On the next row, do not make a stitch to the left of the first top stitch (3) and make a stitch to the right of the last top stitch (4). Continue in the same manner to ensure an identical number of stitches on each row.

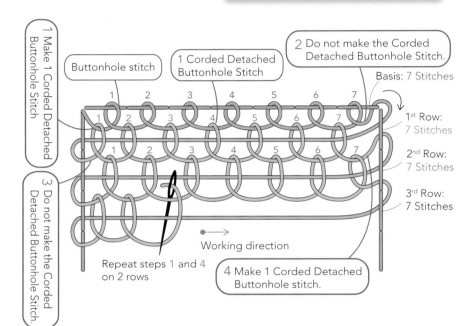

1 Make 1 Corded Detached Buttonhole Stitch

3 Do not make the Corded Detached Buttonhole Stitch.

Buttonhole stitch

1 Corded Detached Buttonhole Stitch

2 Do not make the Corded Detached Buttonhole Stitch.

Basis: 7 Stitches

1st Row: 7 Stitches

2nd Row: 7 Stitches

3rd Row: 7 Stitches

Working direction

Repeat steps 1 and 4 on 2 rows

4 Make 1 Corded Detached Buttonhole stitch.

2 Increasing the Number of Stitches

Embroider the outline of the pattern using back stitch. Sew the basic corded detached buttonhole stitches as above. From the first row, sew one corded detached buttonhole stitch on each side.

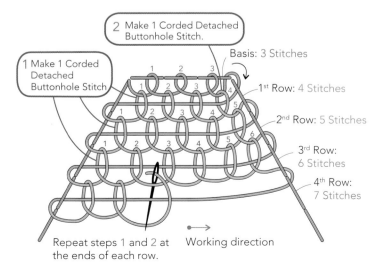

2 Make 1 Corded Detached Buttonhole Stitch.

1 Make 1 Corded Detached Buttonhole Stitch

Basis: 3 Stitches

1st Row: 4 Stitches

2nd Row: 5 Stitches

3rd Row: 6 Stitches

4th Row: 7 Stitches

Repeat steps 1 and 2 at the ends of each row.

Working direction

3 Decreasing the Number of Stitches

Embroider the outline of the pattern using back stitch. Sew the basic corded detached buttonhole stitches as above. From the next row, do not sew one less corded detached buttonhole stitch at the end of the row.

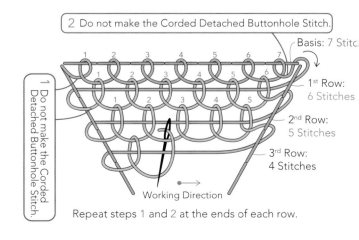

2 Do not make the Corded Detached Buttonhole Stitch.

Basis: 7 Stitc

1 Do not make the Corded Detached Buttonhole Stitch.

1st Row: 6 Stitches

2nd Row: 5 Stitches

3rd Row: 4 Stitches

Working Direction

Repeat steps 1 and 2 at the ends of each row.

※ There is a gap between the stitching and the fabric.

1 Embroider the outline of the pattern using back stitch. Run the needle under the first top back stitch and sew a buttonhole stitch.

Use a blunt tipped needle.

2 Sew another detached buttonhole stitch.

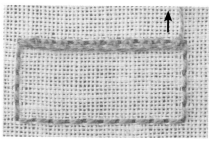

3 Continue to the row in the same manner.

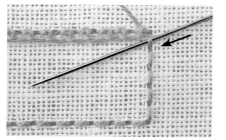

4 Run the needle from the outside to the inside under the first back stitch on the right side.

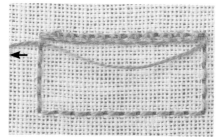

5 Run the needle from the inside to the outside under the first back stitch on the left side.

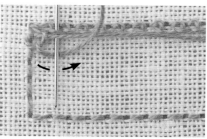

6 Run the needle under the stitch from the previous row and pull the thread to embroider the corded detached buttonhole stitch.

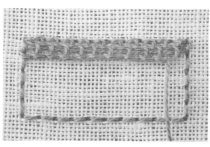

7 Continue to sew corded detached buttonhole stitches in the same way until you get to the right side.

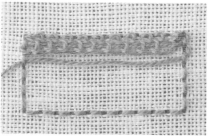

8 Run the needle under the first back stitch on the right side, then run it from the outside to the inside under the second back stitch and tighten the thread.

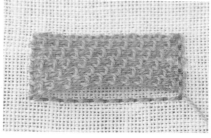

9 Continue embroidering in the same way.

10 Finish off the bottom of the shape by running the needle under the back stitches and corded detached buttonhole stitches. If required, stuff the shape before finishing off (see p. 99).

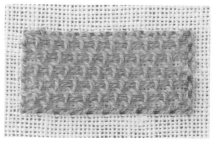

11 The shape has now been completed.

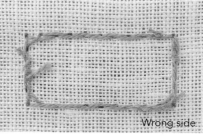

Wrong side

12 View of the wrong side. Only the back stitches are visible on the wrong side.

Buttonhole Bar

Depending on the tension of the support threads, a straight or curved bar can be created.

Actual size

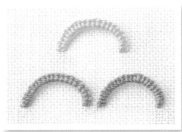

Curved bar with two support threads

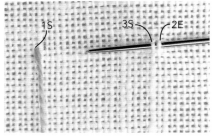

1   Bring out the needle at 1S, insert it at 2E (length is equivalent to the bar), then bring it out at 3S.

2   A support thread has been attached.

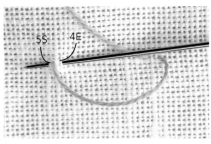

3   Insert the needle at 4E, next to 1, then bring it out at 5S, next to 1.

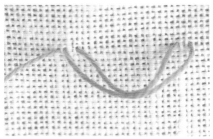

4   Two support threads have been attached. Form them in the shape of the bar (straight or curved).

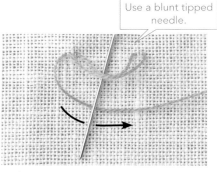

Use a blunt tipped needle.

5   Pull the needle downwards under support threads, then sew a buttonhole stitch.

6   Pull the thread closer to the left side.

7   Continue to sew buttonhole stitches from left to right.

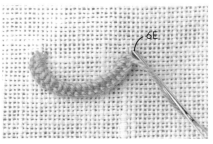

8   Insert the needle at 6E (next to 2) to finish off.

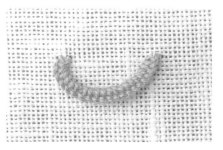

9   The buttonhole bar has been completed.

Detached Buttonhole Stitch

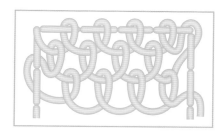

Sew corded detached buttonhole stitches back and forth without pulling the thread taught the rows.

Actual size

※ There is a gap between the stitching and the fabric.

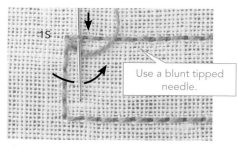

Use a blunt tipped needle.

1 Embroider the outline of the pattern using back stitch. Pull the needle downward under the back stitch and make a corded detached buttonhole stitch.

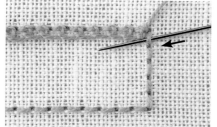

2 At the end of the row, run the needle upwards under the last back stitch from the top side, then from right to left under the first back stitch on the right side.

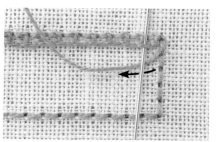

3 Sew corded detached buttonhole stitches from right to left, working the needle under the corded detached buttonhole stitches of the row above.

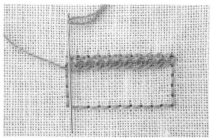

4 Ensure you get the same number of stitches as the previous row.

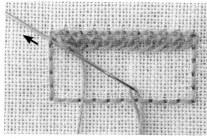

5 Insert the needle from inside to outside under the back stitch in the first row.

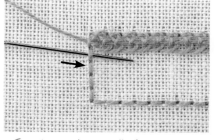

6 Insert the needle from outside to inside under the back stitch of the second row.

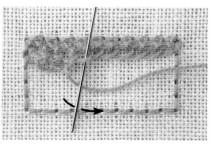

7 Continue to embroider in the same way.

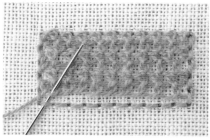

8 Finish off by running the needle under the back stitches and the corded detached buttonhole stitches. If required, stuff before finishing off (see p. 99).

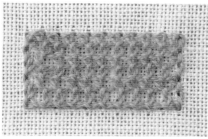

9 The shape has been embroidered using the detached buttonhole stitch.

Detached Buttonhole Stitch

Start by embroidering the outline of the circle using back stitch. Decrease the number of stitches when embroidering in a circle. To do this, divide the outline of the circle in equal parts, then embroider the outline with the back stitch. Sew the corded detached buttonhole stitches of the first round by running the needle under the back stitches (creating the stitches shown in blue). In the second round, run the needle under the stitches of the first round to make corded detached buttonhole stitches (creating the stitches shown in pink). Decrease the number of stitches as you go by skipping one stitch.

Actual size

Run the needle under the back stitches to sew the corded detached buttonhole stitches of the first round (stitches shown in blue). On the second round, run the needle under the stitches of the first round to sew the corded detached buttonhole stitches (stitches shown in pink).

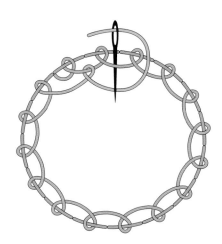

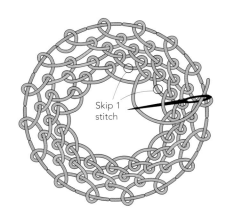

Skip 1 stitch

Stitches and Colors for Patterns D and L, page 86

※ DMC Pearl cotton 8 was used.

Pattern D
1. Divide the outline of the circle into 18 and embroider it using back stitch (3348).
2. Run the needle under the back stitches and sew detached buttonhole stitches (745).
3. Sew two more rounds using detached button stitch, running the needle under the stitches of the previous round.
4. In the fourth round, skip every second stitch to decrease the number of stitches.
5. Insert a piece of felt under the stitches, then finish off the shape.
6. Embroider 12 petals using raised leaf stitch (818).

1. Divide the outline of the circle into 18 and embroider it using the back stitch (725).
2. Run the needle under the back stitches and sew detached buttonhole stitches (725).
3. Sew two more rounds using detached button stitch, running the needle under the stitches of the previous round.
4. In the fourth round, skip every second stitch to decrease the number of stitches.
5. Insert a little carded wool under the stitches, then finish off.
6. Embroider the outer petals using in Turkey work (3865).
7. Embroider three rounds the inner petals using Turkey work.

Full size pattern ※ sth = stitch

Raised leaf sth (p. 98) 818, 12 petals

Embroider 18 back stitches 3348 (p. 21) on the contour, then the detached buttonhole stitch (p. 91) 745

4 rounds at the Smyrna stitch (p. 97) 3865

Embroider 18 back stitches (p. 21) on the contour, then the buttonhole stitch (p. 91) 725

※ There is a gap between the stitch and the fabric.

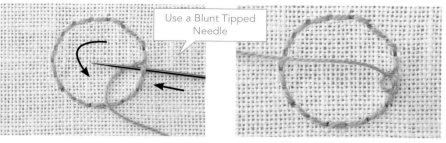

1 Embroider the outline of the pattern using back stitch. Insert the needle from the outside to the inside under the back stitch.

2 Embroider a detached buttonhole stitch.

3 Continue to embroider all around the circle.

4 In the second round, skip the first stitch from the previous round and embroider using detached buttonhole stitch.

5 One stitch decrease has been made.

6 Embroider the other stitches of the second round in the same way.

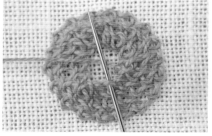

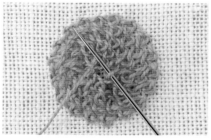

7 Embroider the third round.

8 On the fourth and fifth rounds repeat the sequence, "two detached buttonhole stitches, skip one stitch". Stuff, if necessary (see p. 99).

9 On the sixth round, repeat the sequence "one detached buttonhole stitch, skip one stitch".

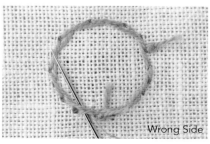

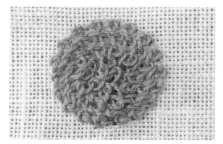

10 Insert the needle at the centre of the circle and bring it out towards the side on the wrong side of the fabric.

11 Finish off on the wrong side of the fabric.

12 The circle has been embroidered in the detached buttonhole stitch.

Raised Stem Stitch

Embroider parallel, long straight stitches as supports, then sew stem stitches to the support. Turn the fabric 180 ° at the end of each row.

※ There is a gap between the stitching and the fabric.

Actual size

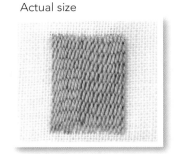

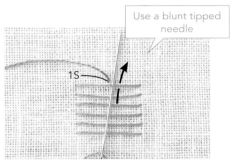

1 Embroider long, parallel straight stitches. Bring out the needle at 1S and pull it upwards under the first straight stitch.

Use a blunt tipped needle

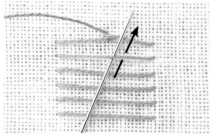

2 Run the needle upward under the second straight stitch and sew in the same way as the stem stitch.

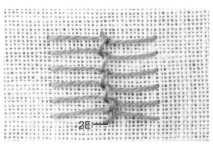

3 Continue to embroider in the same way. At the end of the row, insert the needle at 2E.

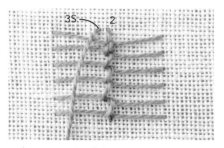

4 Turn the fabric 180 ° so that it is upside down. Bring out the needle at 3S.

5 Repeat steps 2 and 3.

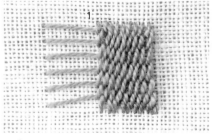

6 Half of the shape has been embroidered.

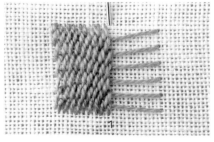

7 Bring out the needle at the centre of the shape.

8 Embroider the other half in the same way.

9 View of the wrong side.

Raised Chain Stitch

Embroider parallel, long straight stitches for the supports, then sew chain stitches on the support.

※ There is a gap between the stitching and the fabric.

Actual size

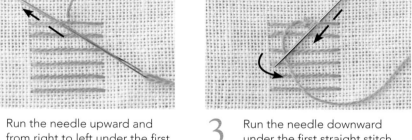

Use a blunt tipped needle

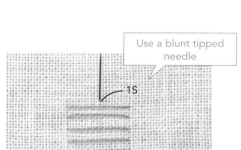

1 Embroider parallel, long stitches. Bring out the needle at 1S.

2 Run the needle upward and from right to left under the first straight stitch.

3 Run the needle downward under the first straight stitch. Pull the thread under the needle.

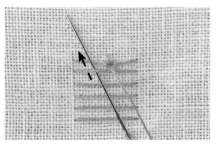

4 Pull the thread tight. The first raised chain stitch has been embroidered.

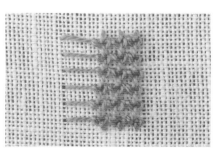

5 Repeat steps 2 to 4.

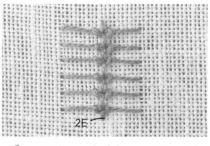

6 At the end of the row, insert the needle at 2E.

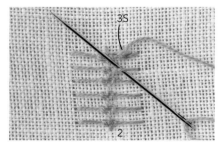

7 Bring out the needle at 3S and embroider the next row in the same way.

8 Half of the shape has been embroidered. Embroider the other half in the same way.

9 The shape has been embroidered using the raised chain stitch.

Ceylon Stitch

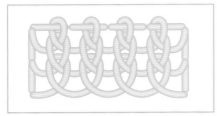

This stitch looks like a knitted jersey. Embroider the stitches from left to right.

Actual size

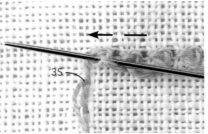

※ There is a gap between the stitching and the fabric.

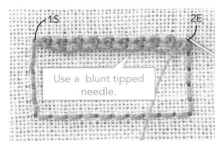

Use a blunt tipped needle.

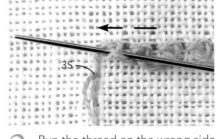

1 Embroider the outline of the pattern using back stitch. Run the needle under the top back stitches and embroider the corded detached buttonhole stitches. At the end of the row, insert the needle at 2E.

2 Run the thread on the wrong side of the fabric and bring out the needle at 3S, at the bottom left of the first back stitch on the left side. Run the needle under the crossing point of the stitch above and embroider a buttonhole stitch.

3 Continue to embroider in the same way.

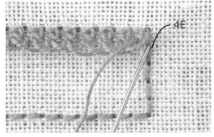

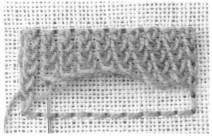

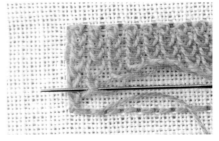

4 At the end of the row, insert the needle at 4E.

5 Run the thread on the wrong side of the fabric. Repeat steps 2 to 4. On the last row, insert the needle under the bottom back stitches.

6 Run the needle under the crossing point of the stitch above.

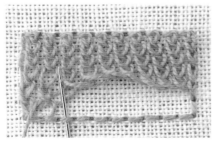

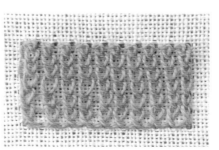

7 To finish off, run the needle under the back stitches on the bottom side.

8 Insert the needle at the bottom right of the pattern to finish.

Turkey Work (Smyrna Stitch)

Actual size

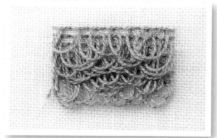

The English name of this stitch comes from the old name of a Turkish city - İzmir (Smyrna).

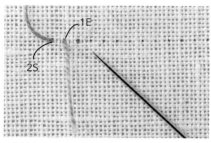

1 Insert the needle at 1E and bring it out at 2S. Leave the thread end on the right side of the fabric.

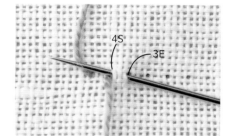

2 Pull the thread upward. Insert the needle at 3E and bring it out at 4S (same place as 1).

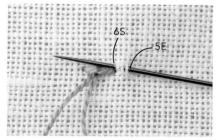

3 Pull the thread down. Insert the needle at 5E and take it out at 6S (same hole as 3). A loop has been formed.

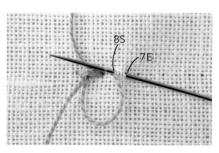

4 Pull the thread upwards. Insert the needle at 7E and bring it out at 8S (same place as 5).

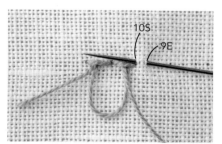

5 Pull the thread down. Insert the needle at 9E and bring it out at 10S (same place as 7). The second loop has been formed.

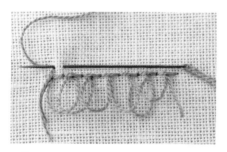

6 Continue to embroider, making sure the loops are the same size. To make several rows, embroider stitches in parallel.

Cutting the loops of the Turkey Work (Smyrna Stitch)

Actual size

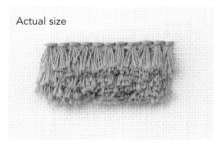

1 Cut the loops of the Turkey work.

2 Trim the threads so they are of equal length.

Raised Leaf Stitch

Sew a raised leaf by working stitches in a triangle.

Actual size

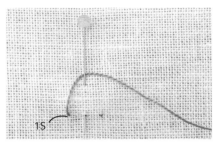

1 Insert a pin in the centre of the leaf. Bring out the needle at 1S.

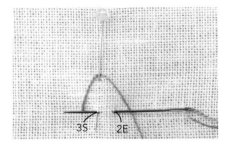

2 Pull the thread round the pin. Insert the needle at 2E and bring it out at 3S.

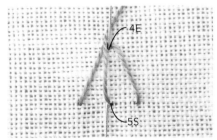

3 Insert the needle at 4E and bring it out in 5S. Pull the thread round the pin. Three support stitches have been sewn.

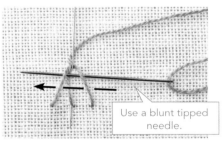

Use a blunt tipped needle.

4 Run the needle from left to right under the two outer stitches.

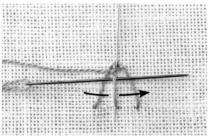

5 Run the needle from left to right under the central support stitch.

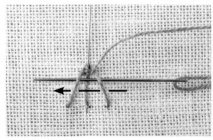

6 Repeat steps 4 and 5. Pull the thread to push the stitches upward.

7 To finish off, insert the needle to the right of the central support stitch.

8 Remove the pin.

9 The raised leaf stitch has now been completed.

Padding

It is possible to stuff the shapes between the fabric and the embroidered stitches.

A: Inserting felt

※ Contrasting colour padding has been used here for demonstration purposes.

1 Cut a piece of felt slightly smaller than the shape. Choose a colour that matches the embroidered shape.

2 Insert the felt under the embroidery stitches using tweezers or an awl.

3 Finish off the embroidered shape running the needle under the back stitches and the detached buttonhole stitches.

B: Inserting Carded Wool

1 Form a ball with carded wool in a colour that matches the thread. Insert the carded wool into the shape while embroidering.

2 Continue to embroider by decreasing the number of stitches. Insert the needle into the centre of the shape and bring it out on the wrong side to finish off.

3 Fasten off the thread on the wrong side of the fabric.

C: Securing Felt Before Embroidery

1 Tack a piece of felt on the fabric (cross in the photo). Embroider five long straight stitches for the support, then fasten off.

Insert the needle into the fabric

2 Insert the needle into the fabric at the ends of the rows. Turn the fabric 180 ° at the end of each row. Remove the tacking as you work.

3 Continue to embroider the rest of the pattern. Bring out the needle on the wrong side of the fabric and fasten off the thread.

DRAWN THREAD WORK AND HARDANGER

DRAWN THREAD WORK

Remove some threads from the fabric and embroider around the remaining threads of the fabric to obtain openwork patterns. This technique was invented in Italy and developed in Europe in the sixteenth century. It has been combined with traditional embroidery from each region. Several variations have resulted, such as Casalguidi from Tuscany, Hedebo from Denmark and Hardanger from Norway, etc.

Pattern p.100

※ DMC 8 pearl cotton has been used. Embroider with thread colour 353, unless otherwise indicated.

Pull the warp threads.

5 threads 4 threads 4 threads 4 threads 14 threads 4 threads 4 threads 4 threads

Satin stitch over 7 threads (p. 110)

Satin stitch over 4 threads (p. 110)

Woven bars over 5 threads (p. 112)

Picots in the centre (p. 113).

Satin stitch over 5 threads (p. 110)

Four sided stitch over 4 threads 842 (p. 108)

Four side stitch over 4 threads (p. 108)

Interlaced border (p. 106)

Four sided stitch over 4 threads (p. 108)

Woven bars over 5 threads (p. 112)

Picots in the centres (p. 113).

Removing Threads

It is important to determine before beginning the embroidery which threads in the fabric are to drawn. The pattern explanations should tell which threads are to be removed.

The length of the threads to be pulled depends on the number of threads to be embroidered in the pattern. For example, to embroider hem stitch (see p. 104), threads are removed in multiples of three.

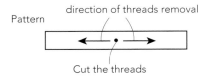

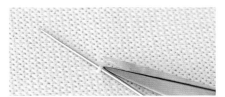

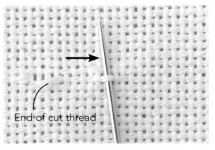

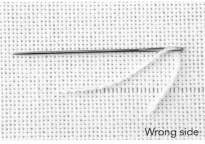

1 Pull the thread from the centre outward. Insert the tip of the needle under the thread and cut it.

2 Use a needle to gradually pull the thread.

3 Turn the fabric on the wrong side. Thread the pulled thread on a needle.

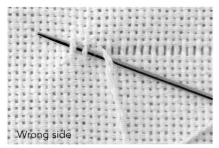

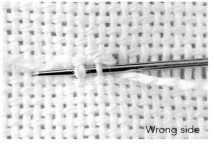

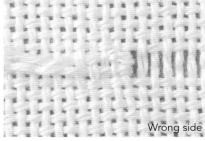

4 Run the needle under two threads on the wrong side of the fabric. Don't cut the end of the thread.

5 Draw the next thread, thread it on a needle and run it under the threads on the fabric.

6 The ends of the thread are run above / below the threads on the fabric.

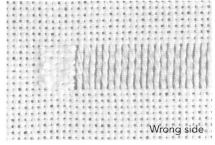

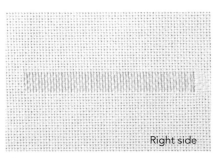

7 Draw the required number of weft threads. Cut the ends of the threads.

8 The threads have been removed.

9 View of the right side with the remaining warp threads.

Securing Drawn Threads

If a large number of threads have drawn, sew buttonhole stitches on the sides to secure your work.

1 Sew buttonhole stitch on the ends of the drawn threads (see p. 38).

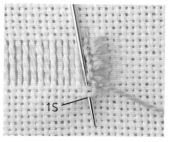

2 Bring out the needle at 1S.

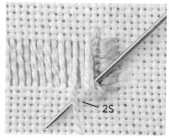

3 Run needle round three threads on the fabric and bring out the needle at 2S (see p.104 for the hem stitch).

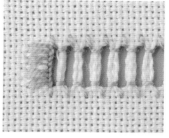

4 The buttonhole stitches and the hem stitch have been completed.

Antique Hem Stitch

This stitch looks like the hem stitch but it is worked on the wrong side of the fabric.

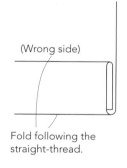

(Wrong side)

Fold following the straight-thread.

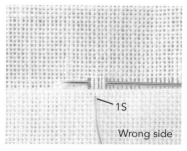

Wrong side

1 Draw the threads (here, 3 werf threads have been drawn). Fold the end of the fabric. Bring out the needle at 1S, under the fold.

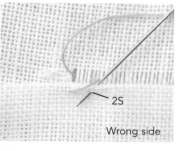

Wrong side

2 Wrap embroidery thread around four warp threads. Insert the needle under the fold of the fabric and bring it out at 2S. Pull the thread down.

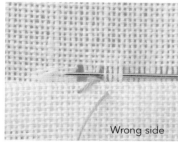

Wrong side

3 Repeat steps 1 and 2. Only the small stitches are visible on the right side.

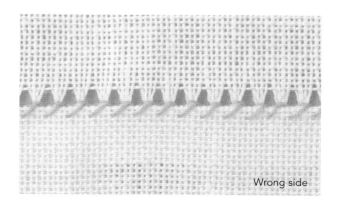

Wrong side

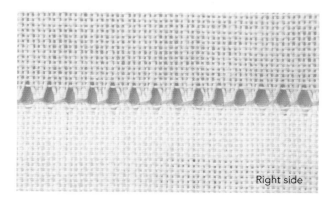

Right side

Hem Stitch

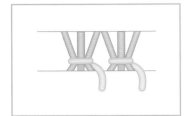

This stitch is the simplest of the hem stitches.

Actual size

Pattern in the picture (3 warp threads per repeat)

Draw the threads from the material in multiples of three (for number of drawn threads, see p. 103).

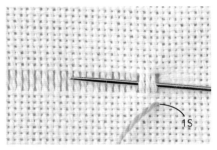

1 Make a stop know and bring out the needle at 1S, slide it under three warp threads.

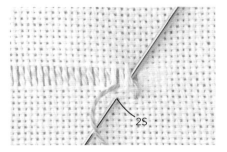

2 Run the needle under the three warp thread, and bring it out at 2S.

3 Pull the thread down.

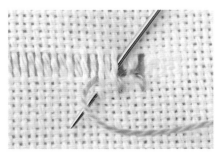

4 Repeat steps 1 and 2.

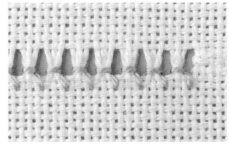

5 Continue to embroider in the same way.

Knotted Border

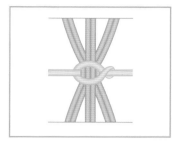

This stitch holds the threads in the centre.

Actual size

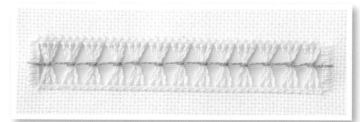

Preparation for pattern in the picture (3 warp threads per repeat)

1 Draw the weft threads (in multiples of 6 warp threads). Weave the ends of the drawn threads (see p. 103).

2 Secure the ends of the drawn threads using buttonhole stitch.

3 Sew hem stitch over 2 warp threads.

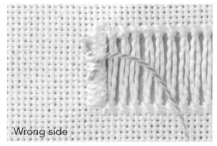

Wrong side

1 Run the end of the thread under the buttonhole stitches on the wrong side of the fabric.

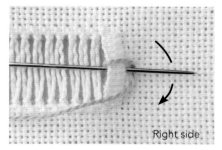

Right side

2 Turn the fabric on the right side. Bring out the needle to the right of the buttonhole stitch. Pull the thread under the needle.

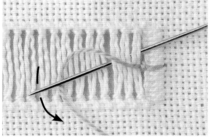

3 Run the needle under three warp threads and pull the thread under the needle.

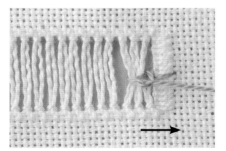

4 Pull the thread towards the right to tighten the knot.

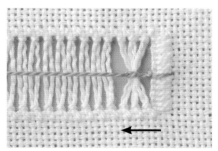

5 Pull the thread to the left (working direction).

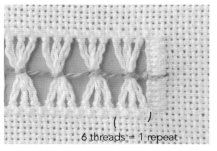

6 threads = 1 repeat

6 Repeat steps 3 to 5.

Interlaced Border

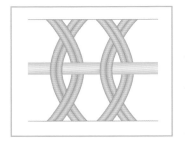

This pattern is made by crossing the warp threads and running the embroidery thread through the centre.

Actual size

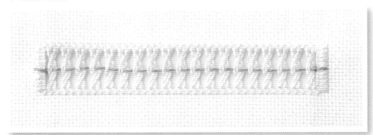

Preparation for the pattern in the picture (4 warp threads per repeat)

1 Draw the weft threads (in multiples of 4 warp threads). Weave the ends of the drawn threads (see p. 103).

2 Secure the ends of the drawn threads using the buttonhole stitch.

3 Sew hem stitch over 2 warp threads.

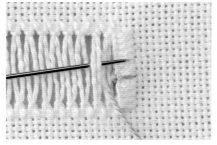

1 Attach the thread to the buttonhole stitches on the wrong side of the fabric (see p. 105, steps 1 to 3). Insert needle under the two warp threads from left to right.

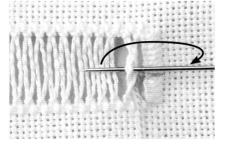

2 Insert needle under the first two warp threads and move the needle from right to left to cross the other two warp threads.

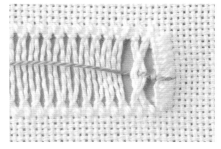

3 Pull the thread. The thread runs through the centre of the cross over.

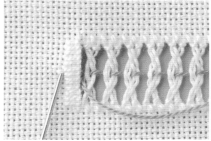

4 Continue to embroider in the same way. Insert the needle in the middle of the buttonhole stitches to finish off.

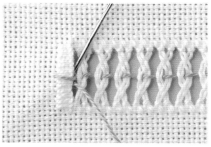

5 Bring out the needle in upward direction. Run it through the stitch just made, then bring it out on the wrong side of the fabric.

6 Work the thread under a few buttonhole stitches to secure it.

Needle Weaving

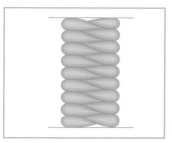

Weaving around the bundles of warp threads.

Actual size

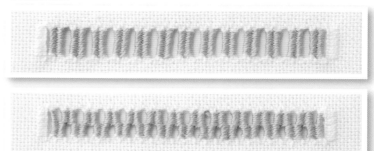

Preparation for the pattern in the picture (6 warp threads per repeat)

1 Draw the weft threads (in multiples of 6 warp threads). Weave the ends of the drawn threads (see p.103).

2 Secure the ends of the drawn threads drawn using the buttonhole stitch.

3 Sew hem stitch over 3 warp threads.

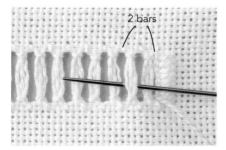

1 Attach the thread to the buttonhole stitches on the wrong side of the fabric. Take the needle to the right of the second bar and run it under the left bar.

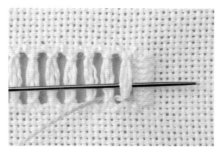

2 Insert the needle in the middle and run it under the right bar.

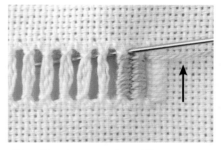

3 Repeat steps 1 and 2 to wrap the thread around the first two bars.

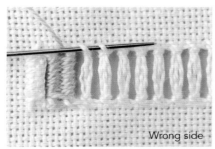

4 Turn the fabric on the wrong side. At the top of the pattern, insert the needle in hem stitch and take it out at the start of the next repeat.

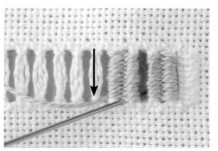

5 Weave the next bar in downward direction.

Changing bar in the middle

Weave the thread around the first two bar to the middle, then weave thread around the second and third bars. Attach the thread and always embroider in upward direction. Continue weaving over just one bar on the last half on the last bar (see p. 108).

Overcast Bar

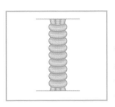

Wrap the thread around the warp threads.

Picture Pattern

Draw the weft threads (in multiples of three warp threads). Sew the hem stitch over three warp threads.

Actual size

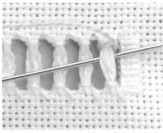

1 Attach the thread on the wrong side of the hem stitch. Wrap the thread around the bar.

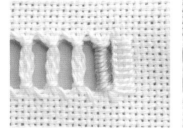

2 Continue winding the thread to the bottom of the bar.

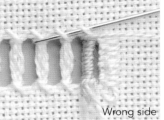

Wrong side

3 Insert the needle on the wrong side of the hem stitches, then bring out the needle on the right side.

4 Wrap the thread from bottom to top around the next bar.

Four Sided Stitch

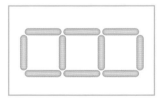

This stitch can also be embroidered without drawing the threads.

Actual size

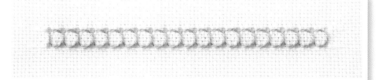

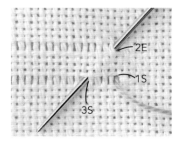

1 Draw the weft threads. Bring out the needle at 1S, insert it at 2E and bring it out at 3S.

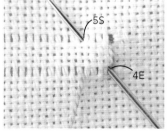

2 Insert the needle at 4E (same place as 1) and bring it out at 5S.

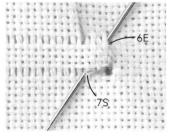

3 Insert the needle at 6S (same place as 2) and bring it out at 7S (same place as 3).

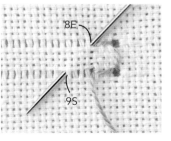

4 Insert the needle at 8E and bring it out at 9S. The first square has been embroidered.

Hardanger

This style of embroidery is the combination of counted stitch and drawn thread embroidery.
It was developed in the south-west of Norway.

Border using
buttonhole
stitch (p. 114)

Dove's eye
(p.112)

Eyelet
stitch
(p.110)

Satin stitch
(p.110)

Picots
(p.113)

Woven bars
(p.112)

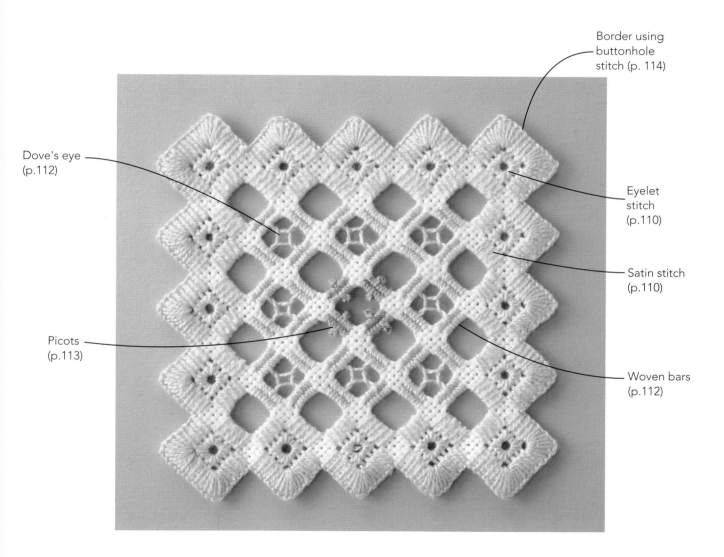

Satin Stitch

Embroider 5 stitches over 4 threads. Embroider in staircase formation. These stitches hold the fabric threads after cutting.

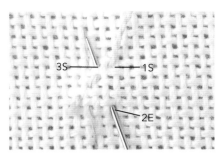

1 To begin, embroider a few running stitches diagonally. Bring out the thread at 1S. Count 4 weft threads, insert the needle at 2E and bring it out at 3S.

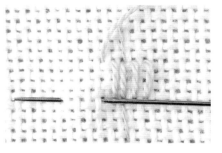

2 Embroider five stitches, then bring out the needle at the next block.

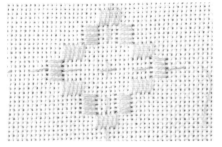

3 Embroider all blocks in the pattern.

Eyelet Stitch

Embroider this stitch inside a frame of satin stitch or buttonhole stitch blocks.
Pull the thread tight to create a hole in the centre.

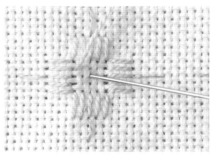

1 Bring out the thread on the inside edge of the blocks and insert the needle in the centre.

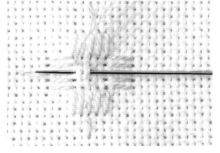

2 Bring out the needle at the next hole in the fabric.

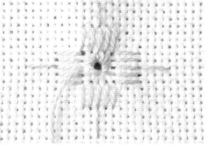

3 Pull the thread tightly and continue to embroider in the same way, turning the fabric as you go.

4 Work the needle under the five stitches on the wrong side.

5 Cut the thread.

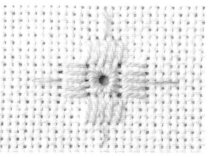

6 The eyelet stitch has been completed.

Interior Openwork

Cut the fabric threads flush with the satin stitch and draw the threads one by one. Be careful not to cut the embroidery thread.

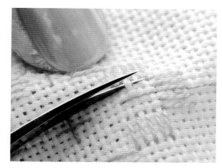

1 Slide the tips of the scissors to next to the satin stitch, then cut one thread of the fabric.

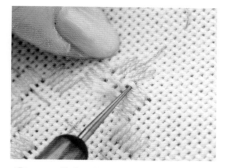

2 Pull the thread using an awl. Draw the other 3 threads.

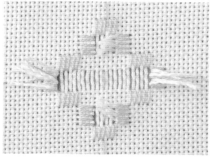

3 The weft threads have been drawn.

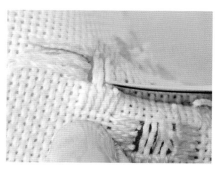

4 Cut the warp threads in the same way.

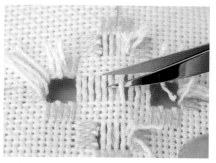

5 Cut the threads one by one, being careful not to cut any other threads.

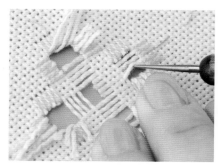

6 Draw the threads one by one.

7 Turn the fabric on the wrong side. Lift the threads and cut them flush with the embroidered stitch.

8 The warp and weft threads have been drawn.

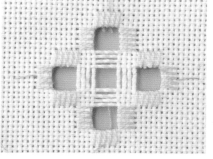

9 The openwork has now been completed.

Woven Bars

Work the threads alternatively over and under the two thread bars. Work back and forth.

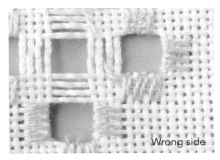

1 Work the needle under the satin stitch block on the wrong side. Bring out the thread in the middle of the four threads on the fabric. View of the wrong side.

Wrong side

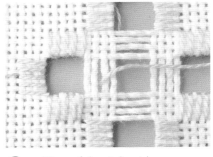

2 View of the right side.

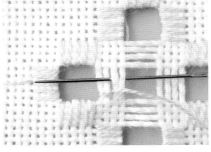

3 Wrap the thread alternately over and under two threads of the bar. Work back and forth.

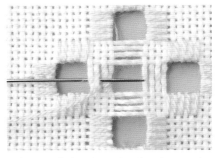

4 Pull the thread tight after each round.

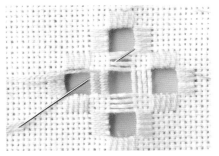

5 At the end of the first bar, bring out the needle in the centre of the next bar.

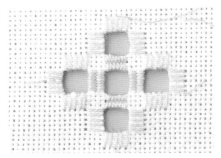

6 The woven bars have now been completed.

Dove's Eye

Use this stitch with woven bars.

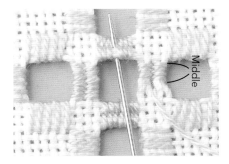

1 Embroider the last woven bar to the middle. Bring out the needle in the middle of the neighbouring bar.

Middle

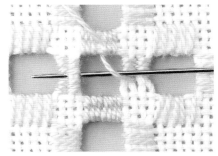

2 Run the needle under the thread worked in step 1 and bring it out in the middle of the neighboring bar.

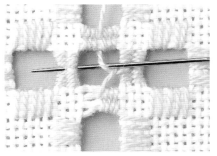

3 Rotate the fabric 90°. Run the needle under the thread worked in step 2 and bring it out in the middle of the neighbouring bar.

cont. →

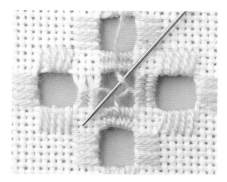

4 Rotate the fabric 90°. Run the needle under the thread worked in step 3.

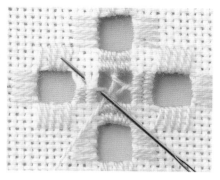

5 Run the needle under the thread worked in step, then complete the woven bar.

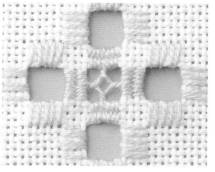

6 The dove's eye has been completed.

Picots

Use the picots with woven bars.

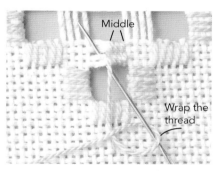

1 Embroider the woven bars to the middle. Wrap the thread once around the needle, then bring it out in the middle of the bar.

2 Pull the thread to tighten it around the needle. Hold the picot and remove the needle.

3 Rotate the fabric 180 °. Insert the needle in the middle of the bar, then wrap the thread once around the needle.

4 Two picots have been created.

5 Complete the woven bar.

6 Embroider the three other woven bars using picots.

Buttonhole Stitch

Use this stitch to make the border of your work. Insert the needle several times into the same place to form the corner.

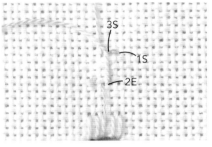

1 To start, embroider a few running stitches diagonally. Bring out the thread at 1S. Insert the needle at 2E and bring it out at 3S. Pull the thread under the needle.

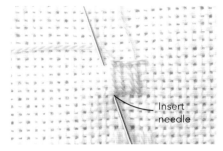

2 Continue to embroider in the same way without leaving gaps.

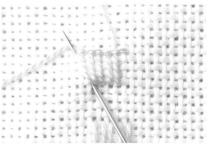

3 To embroider the corner, insert the needle in the same place and bring it out one thread further on.

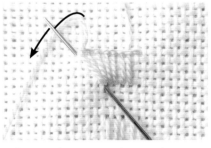

4 At the corner, change the direction of work.

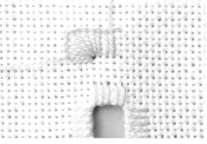

5 The corner has now been embroidered.

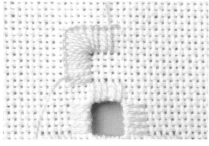

6 Embroider five buttonhole stitches per block.

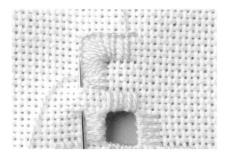

7 Change the direction of work and keep embroidering the buttonhole stitch.

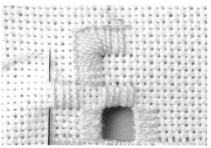

8 Embroider one block, then repeat steps 2 to 7 to embroider the border.

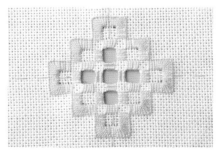

9 The buttonhole stitch is now completed.

Cutting the Border

Cut the threads of the fabric flush with the buttonhole stitches, while being careful not to cut the embroidery thread.

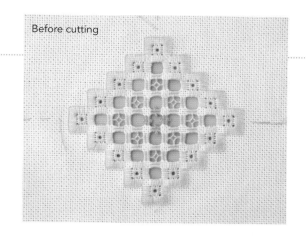
Before cutting

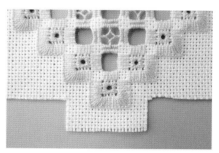

1 Cut the outline of the work about 1cm from the edge of the buttonhole stitch.

2 Draw the threads one by one.

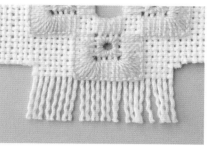

3 The weft threads have been drawn to the level of the embroidered stitches.

Wrong side

4 Cut the warp threads one by one flush with the buttonhole stitches.

Wrong side

5 View of the wrong side.

Wrong side

6 View of the right side. The end of the fabric threads is not visible.

Wrong side

7 Cut the threads of the next edge.

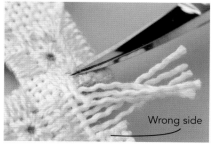
Wrong side

8 Cut the threads flush with the stitches.

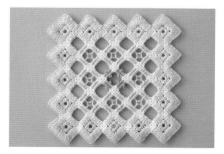

9 Cut the threads of the other edges in the same way. The work has been completed.

Small Pattern Sampler

These patterns are embroidered with the stitches presented in this book.

Plants

※ These patterns are embroidered with DMC Stranded cotton thread.
※ See p. 127 to understand how to read the patterns.

Violette

Pansy

Lily of the valley

Dandelion

Scabious

Acorn

Olives

Bunch of grapes

Full Size Patterns

※ These patterns are embroidered with DMC Mouline Special 25 cotton thread.
※ See p. 127 to understand how to read the patterns.

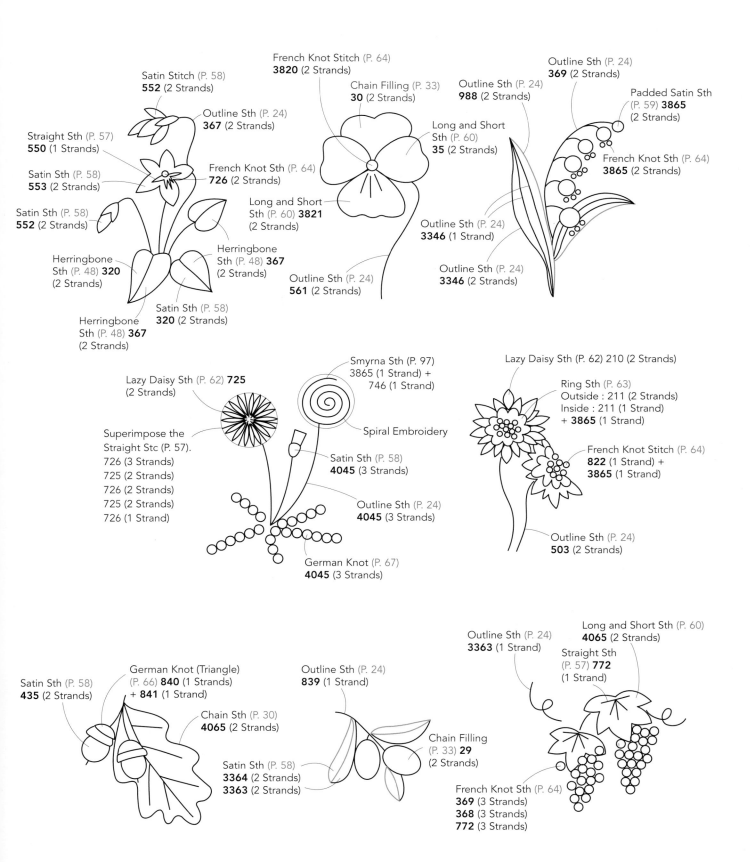

Satin Stitch (P. 58)
552 (2 Strands)

Outline Sth (P. 24)
367 (2 Strands)

Straight Sth (P. 57)
550 (1 Strands)

Satin Sth (P. 58)
553 (2 Strands)

Satin Sth (P. 58)
552 (2 Strands)

French Knot Sth (P. 64)
726 (2 Strands)

Herringbone
Sth (P. 48) **320**
(2 Strands)

Herringbone
Sth (P. 48) **367**
(2 Strands)

Satin Sth (P. 58)
320 (2 Strands)

Herringbone
Sth (P. 48) **367**
(2 Strands)

French Knot Stitch (P. 64)
3820 (2 Strands)

Chain Filling (P. 33)
30 (2 Strands)

Long and Short
Sth (P. 60)
35 (2 Strands)

Long and Short
Sth (P. 60) **3821**
(2 Strands)

Outline Sth (P. 24)
561 (2 Strands)

Outline Sth (P. 24)
988 (2 Strands)

Outline Sth (P. 24)
369 (2 Strands)

Padded Satin Sth
(P. 59) **3865**
(2 Strands)

French Knot Sth (P. 64)
3865 (2 Strands)

Outline Sth (P. 24)
3346 (1 Strand)

Outline Sth (P. 24)
3346 (2 Strands)

Lazy Daisy Sth (P. 62) **725**
(2 Strands)

Superimpose the
Straight Stc (P. 57).
726 (3 Strands)
725 (2 Strands)
726 (2 Strands)
725 (2 Strands)
726 (1 Strand)

Smyrna Sth (P. 97)
3865 (1 Strand) +
746 (1 Strand)

Spiral Embroidery

Satin Sth (P. 58)
4045 (3 Strands)

Outline Sth (P. 24)
4045 (3 Strands)

German Knot (P. 67)
4045 (3 Strands)

Lazy Daisy Sth (P. 62) 210 (2 Strands)

Ring Sth (P. 63)
Outside : 211 (2 Strands)
Inside : 211 (1 Strand)
+ **3865** (1 Strand)

French Knot Stitch (P. 64)
822 (1 Strand) +
3865 (1 Strand)

Outline Sth (P. 24)
503 (2 Strands)

Satin Sth (P. 58)
435 (2 Strands)

German Knot (Triangle)
(P. 66) **840** (1 Strands)
+ **841** (1 Strand)

Chain Sth (P. 30)
4065 (2 Strands)

Satin Sth (P. 58)
3364 (2 Strands)
3363 (2 Strands)

Outline Sth (P. 24)
839 (1 Strand)

Chain Filling
(P. 33) **29**
(2 Strands)

Outline Sth (P. 24)
3363 (1 Strand)

Long and Short Sth (P. 60)
4065 (2 Strands)

Straight Sth
(P. 57) **772**
(1 Strand)

French Knot Sth (P. 64)
369 (3 Strands)
368 (3 Strands)
772 (3 Strands)

Plants and Insects

※ These patterns are embroidered with DMC Stranded 25 cotton thread.

※ See p. 127 to understand how to read the patterns.

Four-leaf clover

Ladybird

Rose

Beetle

Bee

Cherry blossoms

Forget-me-not

Daisy

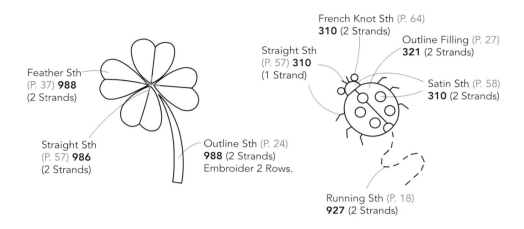

Feather Sth (P. 37) **988** (2 Strands)

Straight Sth (P. 57) **986** (2 Strands)

Outline Sth (P. 24) **988** (2 Strands) Embroider 2 Rows.

French Knot Sth (P. 64) **310** (2 Strands)

Straight Sth (P. 57) **310** (1 Strand)

Outline Filling (P. 27) **321** (2 Strands)

Satin Sth (P. 58) **310** (2 Strands)

Running Sth (P. 18) **927** (2 Strands)

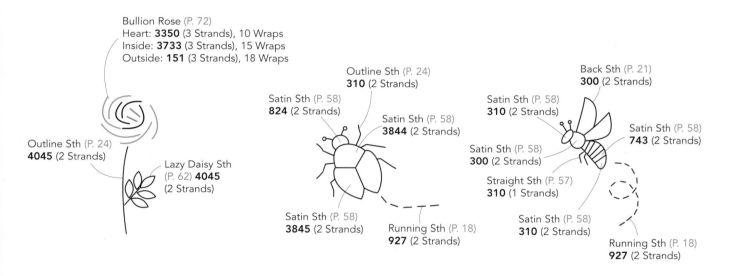

Bullion Rose (P. 72)
Heart: **3350** (3 Strands), 10 Wraps
Inside: **3733** (3 Strands), 15 Wraps
Outside: **151** (3 Strands), 18 Wraps

Outline Sth (P. 24) **4045** (2 Strands)

Lazy Daisy Sth (P. 62) **4045** (2 Strands)

Satin Sth (P. 58) **824** (2 Strands)

Outline Sth (P. 24) **310** (2 Strands)

Satin Sth (P. 58) **3844** (2 Strands)

Satin Sth (P. 58) **3845** (2 Strands)

Running Sth (P. 18) **927** (2 Strands)

Satin Sth (P. 58) **310** (2 Strands)

Satin Sth (P. 58) **300** (2 Strands)

Straight Sth (P. 57) **310** (1 Strands)

Back Sth (P. 21) **300** (2 Strands)

Satin Sth (P. 58) **743** (2 Strands)

Satin Sth (P. 58) **310** (2 Strands)

Running Sth (P. 18) **927** (2 Strands)

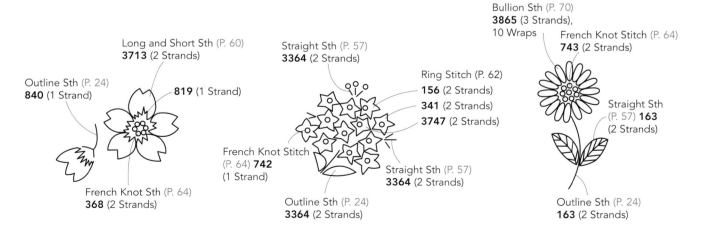

Outline Sth (P. 24) **840** (1 Strand)

Long and Short Sth (P. 60) **3713** (2 Strands)

819 (1 Strand)

French Knot Sth (P. 64) **368** (2 Strands)

Straight Sth (P. 57) **3364** (2 Strands)

Ring Stitch (P. 62) **156** (2 Strands)
341 (2 Strands)
3747 (2 Strands)

French Knot Stitch (P. 64) **742** (1 Strand)

Outline Sth (P. 24) **3364** (2 Strands)

Straight Sth (P. 57) **3364** (2 Strands)

Bullion Sth (P. 70) **3865** (3 Strands), 10 Wraps

French Knot Stitch (P. 64) **743** (2 Strands)

Straight Sth (P. 57) **163** (2 Strands)

Outline Sth (P. 24) **163** (2 Strands)

A

B

C

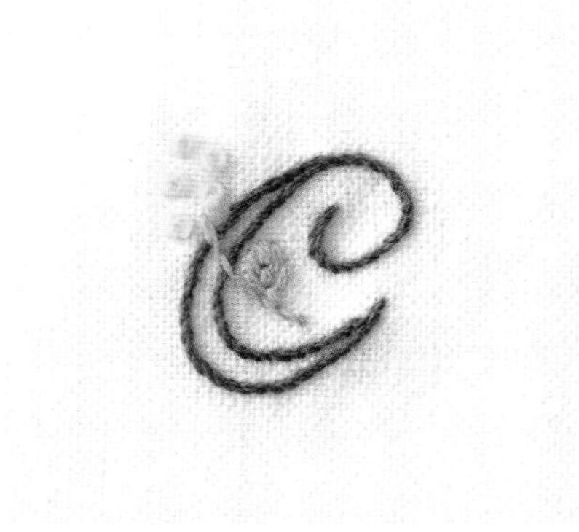

D

E

F

G

H

I

J

K

L

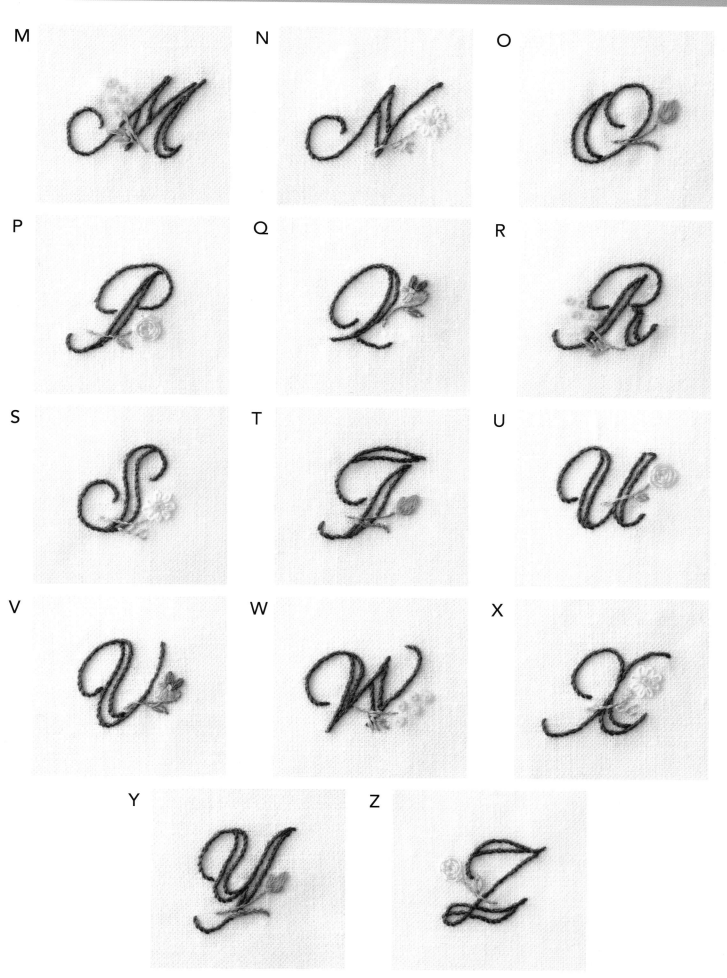

M   N   O

P   Q   R

S   T   U

V   W   X

Y   Z

Alphabet

Embroider The Letters On The Stitch (P. 24) **838** (2 Strands).

※These patterns are embroidered with DMC Mouline Special 25 cotton thread.

※See p. 127 to understand how to read the patterns.

Full Size Patterns

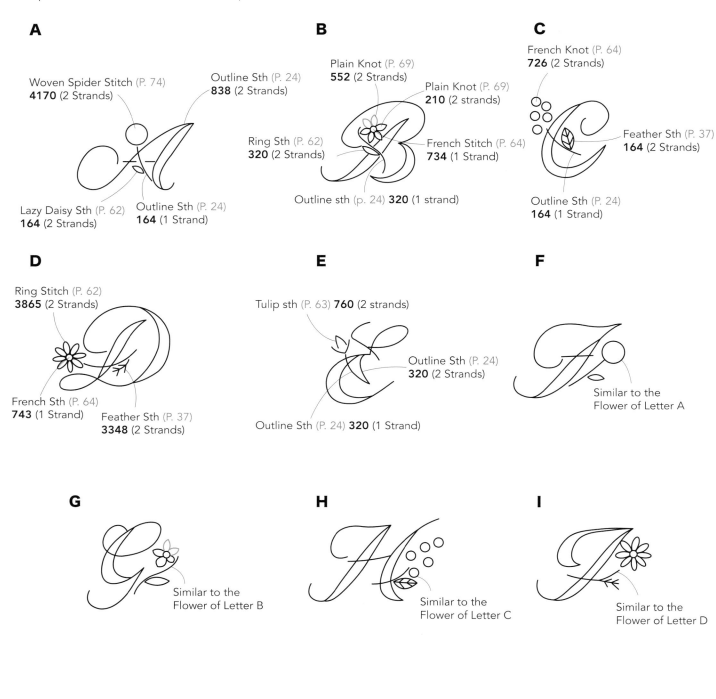

A

Woven Spider Stitch (P. 74) **4170** (2 Strands)

Outline Sth (P. 24) **838** (2 Strands)

Lazy Daisy Sth (P. 62) **164** (2 Strands)

Outline Sth (P. 24) **164** (1 Strand)

B

Plain Knot (P. 69) **552** (2 Strands)

Plain Knot (P. 69) **210** (2 strands)

Ring Sth (P. 62) **320** (2 Strands)

French Stitch (P. 64) **734** (1 Strand)

Outline sth (p. 24) **320** (1 strand)

C

French Knot (P. 64) **726** (2 Strands)

Feather Sth (P. 37) **164** (2 Strands)

Outline Sth (P. 24) **164** (1 Strand)

D

Ring Stitch (P. 62) **3865** (2 Strands)

French Sth (P. 64) **743** (1 Strand)

Feather Sth (P. 37) **3348** (2 Strands)

E

Tulip sth (P. 63) **760** (2 strands)

Outline Sth (P. 24) **320** (2 Strands)

Outline Sth (P. 24) **320** (1 Strand)

F

Similar to the Flower of Letter A

G

Similar to the Flower of Letter B

H

Similar to the Flower of Letter C

I

Similar to the Flower of Letter D

J

Similar to the Flower of Letter E

K

Similar to the Flower of Letter A

L

Similar to the Flower of Letter B

M

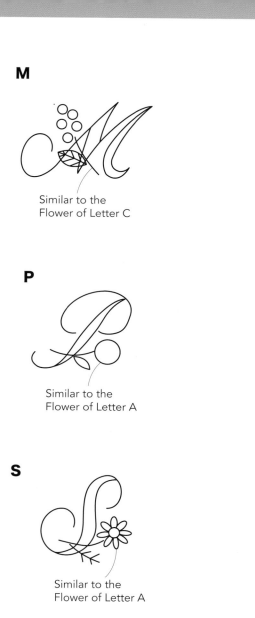

Similar to the
Flower of Letter C

N

Similar to the
Flower of Letter D

O

Similar to the
Flower of Letter E

P

Similar to the
Flower of Letter A

Q

Similar to the
Flower of Letter B

R

Similar to the
Flower of Letter C

S

Similar to the
Flower of Letter A

T

Similar to the
Flower of Letter E

U

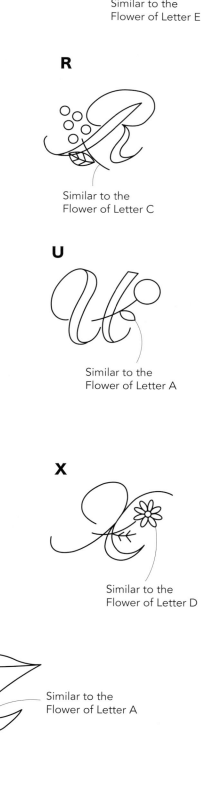

Similar to the
Flower of Letter A

V

Similar to the
Flower of Letter B

W

Similar to the
Flower of Letter C

X

Similar to the
Flower of Letter D

Y

Similar to the
Flower of Letter E

Z

Similar to the
Flower of Letter A

More About Embroidery

A presentation of the history of embroidery, the names of the stitches and various styles of embroidery for further appreciation of this handicraft.

History of Embroidery

Embroidery is believed to go back to prehistoric times, when humans began to dress in clothing made from animal skins. The technique of assembling the pieces of skin using a bone needle is said to be the origin of sewing and embroidery. This art is rooted in life and most of the stitches currently known would have been invented before our times. It is unknown where embroidery originated but one could suppose that the techniques, like the other skills, were transferred from ancient Egypt and the Roman Empire to Europe and from the Middle East to Asia and Europe. Until the sixteenth century, embroidery was carried out in workshops by artisans. However, with world trade and the movement of people, each region has appropriated these skills by adapting them to handicrafts.

Linear Stitches

The choice of stitches for embroidering a pattern may vary depending on the time and region. Linear embroidery has developed particularly in Islamic culture. The prohibition of idolatry among Muslims influenced the birth of decorative and abstract arts, like the arabesque. Patterns are often made in running stitch, Holbein stitch, back stitch and split stitch. Holbein stitch was transferred from Spain and Italy, then developed in Europe.

Chain Stitch

Chain stitch has been common in various regions and eras. This stitch was mainly used in Ancient Egypt and China. In the eighteenth century, variations, such as the twisted chain stitch and the double chain stitch, appeared and were often combined with laced herringbone stitch. These stitches remain popular these days.

Cross Stitch

Cross stitch appeared in Europe after the sixteenth century and was fashionable in the seventeenth and eighteenth century. The elongated cross stitch and half cross stitch are also common and used to embroider larger or smaller surfaces. Canvas embroidery was invented in England. The cross stitch and half cross stitch are embroidered with wool on a loose weft linen fabric. In Austria and Germany, tapestries were made with small stitches on a silk canvas representing landscapes and pastoral scenes.

Satin Stitch

Goblin stitch is embroidered in straight lines to fill a surface. It appeared around the thirteenth century. The satin stitch and the encroaching satin stitch came into being around the fifteenth century and are embroidered without necessarily following straight lines. These stitches have been subject to variations and have developed into techniques, such as silk shading and needle painting.

Couching

Couching is one of the oldest stitches. Evidence of this stitch have been found on objects from the first century BC. The Scythians, the ancient nomadic people of Eurasia, were used this stitch. After the fourteenth century, it was used in German white work. Much of this German work was embroidered in convents. From the fifteenth to the eighteenth century, this stitch was used to attach expensive gold and silk threads to the fabric, where the gold threads are held in place by coloured silk threads give the work texture.

Assisi Embroidery

This technique was invented in Assisi, Italy. The outline of the patterns is embroidered using Holbein stitch and the interior is left untouched. The outer pattern is embroidered in cross stitch. The oldest existing work dates back to the sixteenth century. The patterns representing birds and animals etc. are embroidered with red thread. Some works are also embroidered with green, blue or brown thread.

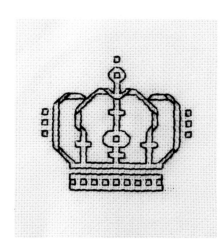

Blackwork

This technique of Moorish origin came to England via Spain, following the marriage of Henry VIII and Catherine of Aragon. It was very fashionable in England in the sixteenth century.

Before then, this technique had been used in Spain to decorate cuffs and collars. It is therefore sometimes called "Spanish work".

The patterns are embroidered in Holbein stitch with black thread. In the sixteenth century, geometric patterns combined with plants were popular. The works of the nineteenth and twentieth centuries were more nuanced with more or less dense stitches representing shadows.

Richelieu Embroidery

The outlines of the patterns are embroidered using buttonhole stitch and the interior is then cut to obtain a serrated pattern.

This technique, used in the twelfth century in Germany and Italy, influenced the rise of needle lace and bobbin lace.

The patterns using this type of embroidery are more solid than those of other techniques. According the fashion for lace in sixteenth century Europe, Richelieu embroidery patterns were used instead of lace. The patterns adorning the clothes worn by royal court officials and clergymen were as delicate as lace.

Cover and Chapter Full Size Patterns

※ These patterns are embroidered with DMC Stranded cotton thread, unless otherwise stated.

※ Embroider the rose using cast-on stitch and the bud with one thread of Special Embroider No 25 cotton.

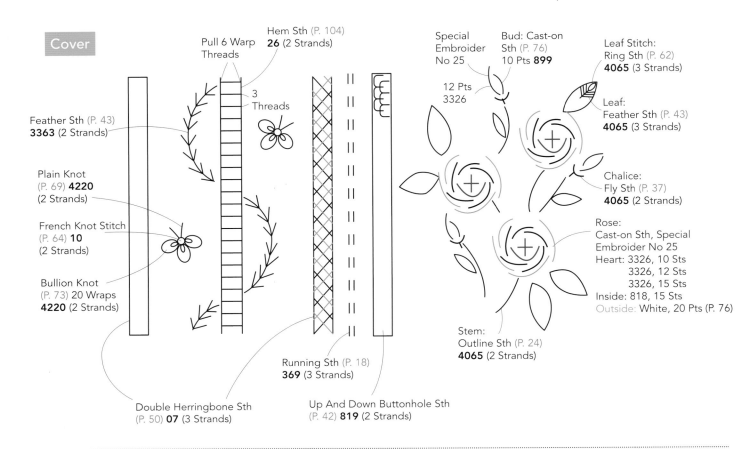

Cover

Pull 6 Warp Threads

Hem Sth (P. 104) **26** (2 Strands)

3 Threads

Feather Sth (P. 43) **3363** (2 Strands)

Plain Knot (P. 69) **4220** (2 Strands)

French Knot Stitch (P. 64) **10** (2 Strands)

Bullion Knot (P. 73) 20 Wraps **4220** (2 Strands)

Double Herringbone Sth (P. 50) **07** (3 Strands)

Running Sth (P. 18) **369** (3 Strands)

Up And Down Buttonhole Sth (P. 42) **819** (2 Strands)

Special Embroidery No 25
12 Pts 3326

Bud: Cast-on Sth (P. 76) 10 Pts **899**

Leaf Stitch: Ring Sth (P. 62) **4065** (3 Strands)

Leaf: Feather Sth (P. 43) **4065** (3 Strands)

Chalice: Fly Sth (P. 37) **4065** (2 Strands)

Rose:
Cast-on Sth, Special Embroidery No 25
Heart: 3326, 10 Sts
 3326, 12 Sts
 3326, 15 Sts
Inside: 818, 15 Sts
Outside: White, 20 Pts (P. 76)

Stem: Outline Sth (P. 24) **4065** (2 Strands)

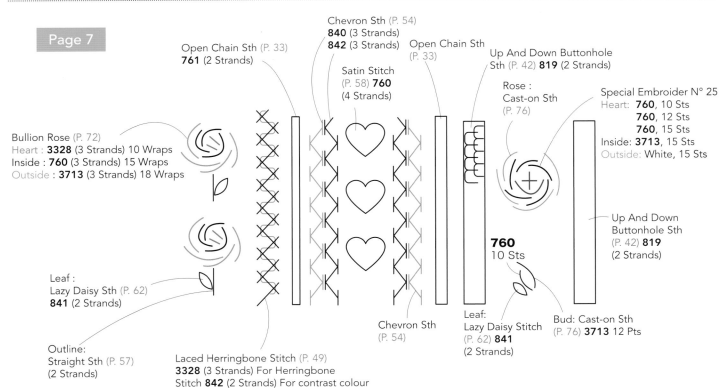

Page 7

Bullion Rose (P. 72)
Heart : **3328** (3 Strands) 10 Wraps
Inside : **760** (3 Strands) 15 Wraps
Outside : **3713** (3 Strands) 18 Wraps

Open Chain Sth (P. 33) **761** (2 Strands)

Chevron Sth (P. 54) **840** (3 Strands) **842** (3 Strands)

Satin Stitch (P. 58) **760** (4 Strands)

Open Chain Sth (P. 33)

Up And Down Buttonhole Sth (P. 42) **819** (2 Strands)

Rose : Cast-on Sth (P. 76)

Special Embroider N° 25
Heart: **760**, 10 Sts
 760, 12 Sts
 760, 15 Sts
Inside: **3713**, 15 Sts
Outside: White, 15 Sts

Up And Down Buttonhole Sth (P. 42) **819** (2 Strands)

Leaf : Lazy Daisy Sth (P. 62) **841** (2 Strands)

Outline: Straight Sth (P. 57) (2 Strands)

Laced Herringbone Stitch (P. 49) **3328** (3 Strands) For Herringbone Stitch **842** (2 Strands) For contrast colour

Chevron Sth (P. 54)

760 10 Sts

Leaf: Lazy Daisy Stitch (P. 62) **841** (2 Strands)

Bud: Cast-on Sth (P. 76) **3713** 12 Pts

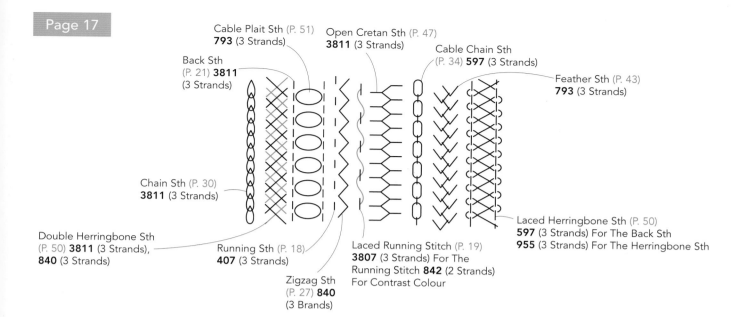

Cable Plait Sth (P. 51)
793 (3 Strands)

Open Cretan Sth (P. 47)
3811 (3 Strands)

Cable Chain Sth
(P. 34) **597** (3 Strands)

Back Sth
(P. 21) **3811**
(3 Strands)

Feather Sth (P. 43)
793 (3 Strands)

Chain Sth (P. 30)
3811 (3 Strands)

Laced Herringbone Sth (P. 50)
597 (3 Strands) For The Back Sth
955 (3 Strands) For The Herringbone Sth

Double Herringbone Sth
(P. 50) **3811** (3 Strands),
840 (3 Strands)

Running Sth (P. 18)
407 (3 Strands)

Laced Running Stitch (P. 19)
3807 (3 Strands) For The
Running Stitch **842** (2 Strands)
For Contrast Colour

Zigzag Sth
(P. 27) **840**
(3 Brands)

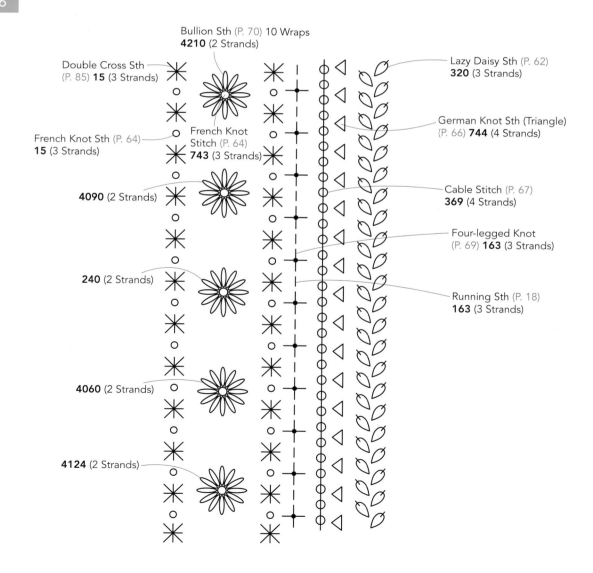

Bullion Sth (P. 70) 10 Wraps
4210 (2 Strands)

Double Cross Sth
(P. 85) **15** (3 Strands)

Lazy Daisy Sth (P. 62)
320 (3 Strands)

French Knot Sth (P. 64)
15 (3 Strands)

French Knot
Stitch (P. 64)
743 (3 Strands)

German Knot Sth (Triangle)
(P. 66) **744** (4 Strands)

4090 (2 Strands)

Cable Stitch (P. 67)
369 (4 Strands)

Four-legged Knot
(P. 69) **163** (3 Strands)

240 (2 Strands)

Running Sth (P. 18)
163 (3 Strands)

4060 (2 Strands)

4124 (2 Strands)

Tuva Publishing

www.tuvapublishing.com

Address Merkez Mah. Cavusbasi Cad. No: 71

Cekmekoy - Istanbul 34782 / Turkey

Tel: +9 0216 642 62 62

The Essential Book of Embroidery Stitches

First Print 2021 / October

All Global Copyrights Belong To
Tuva Tekstil ve Yayıncılık Ltd.

Content Embroidery

Editor in Chief Ayhan DEMİRPEHLİVAN

Project Editor Kader DEMİRPEHLİVAN

Technical Editors Leyla ARAS

Text Editor Catherine VENNER

Graphic Designers Ömer ALP, Abdullah BAYRAKÇI,
Tarık TOKGÖZ, Yunus GÜLDOĞAN

ISBN 978-605-7834-18-8

Lady Boutique Series No.4604
Shishu no Stitch to Kihon
Copyright © Boutique-sha, Inc. 2018
Original Japanese edition published in Japan by Boutique-sha, Inc.
English translation rights arranged with Boutique-sha, Inc.

 **TuvaYayincilik**  **TuvaPublishing**
 **TuvaYayincilik** **TuvaPublishing**

{ Atelier Fil }

Behind the Atelier Fil brand, created in 2004, hides a duo of designers, Hiroko Sei and Shizue Yasui, whose embroidery works in relief are very popular.

Their colorful and delicate patterns are much appreciated.

They regularly participate in exhibitions and teach their technique in various cultural centers in Japan.

http://www.atelier-fil.com